Divorce Proceedings in Illinois

What You Need to Know

D1452769

Mark D. Brent

DISCARD
Hudson Area Public Library
Hudson, IL 61748

25.00

©2012 Thomson Reuters/Aspatore
All rights reserved. Printed in the United States of America.

No part of this publication may be reproduced or distributed in any form or by any means, or stored in a database or retrieval system, except as permitted under Sections 107 or 108 of the U.S. Copyright Act, without prior written permission of the publisher. This book is printed on acid-free paper.

Material in this book is for educational purposes only. This book is sold with the understanding that neither any of the authors nor the publisher is engaged in rendering legal, accounting, investment, or any other professional service as a part of this book. Neither the publisher nor the authors assume any liability for any errors or omissions or for how this book or its contents are used or interpreted or for any consequences resulting directly or indirectly from the use of this book. For legal advice or any other, please consult your personal lawyer or the appropriate professional.

The views expressed by the individuals in this book (or the individuals on the cover) do not necessarily reflect the views shared by the companies they are employed by (or the companies mentioned in this book). The employment status and affiliations of authors with the companies referenced are subject to change.

For additional copies or customer service inquiries, please e-mail west.customer.service@thomson.com.

ISBN 978-0-314-28583-6

Mat #41347021

DEDICATION

This book is dedicated:
With thanks, to my assistant, Phyllis;
With pride, to my family: Robert and Janice, Cameron and
Robert, and Ann, Joe, Courtney, Morgan and Braden, and
With love, to Krissy.

Hudson Area Public Library
Hudson DISCARD

CONTENTS

Introduction:
Reassurance to the Reader

Thank you for picking up this book. My purpose is to provide you with information to help guide your thinking about this important topic. This is not intended to be a textbook, nor is it intended to be a comprehensive resource. Rather, this is intended to be an introduction, a "guided tour," to introduce you to this complex and greatly misunderstood topic. A full discussion of each of the topics addressed here could fill a book this size. The whole of this book would turn into an encyclopedia; so please keep in mind, this book is designed to be a "quick preview," and not an exhaustive discussion of this complicated area of law.

It is a subject that many people find hard to talk about, and even harder to discuss. As such, thank you again, and I hope that you will find this helpful.

Furthermore, the contents of this book do not constitute legal advice. The information provided herein is given strictly for informational and educational purposes. By your purchase of this book, no attorney/client privilege or relationship is being formed. It is strongly suggested that, before you proceed with a divorce or any other legal action regarding your marriage, you obtain the advice of a qualified attorney in your jurisdiction.

In a span of roughly forty years (from the 1960s through the 1990s), the attitude toward divorce in the United States changed drastically. The social and cultural acceptance and attitude toward divorce evolved; from divorce being an unusual and often scandalous event, to being almost commonplace. Whereas divorces were once a rarity, now most of us are familiar with the media's report that somewhere over half of new marriages now end in divorce.

In my 1970s grade school, a classmate whose family was going through a divorce was rare. Of all my childhood friends, none of them lived in a home touched by divorce. I know from personal and direct professional experience that my sons (who attended the same grade school at the turn of the millennium) cannot say the same. In fact, at one point, one of my sons noticed how unusual it was that so many of his friend's parents had *not* divorced.

Popular media reflected people's changing attitudes toward divorce. In the 1960s and 1970s, to have a show like the *Brady Bunch*, parents would have to die mysteriously and pretty much without explanation, to create a blended family. Most would say that our current, more open view of divorce represents a positive step forward, although I have had more than a few clients who would have preferred Mike and Carol Brady's "vanishing spouse" model. Television shows were very slow to accept the idea of divorce. The *Mary Tyler Moore Show* was to be the first show with a divorced lead character, but the network did not want the public to think her character had divorced her former, beloved co-star, Dick Van Dyke.

As America came to grips with the idea of divorce itself being okay, the focus of anxiety became the inevitable fallout of many divorces—custodial battles such as that in *Kramer vs. Kramer*. While post-millennial popular media now accepts divorce more as a common (if not "normal") occurrence, pop culture still reflects our culture's ambivalence about divorce (just how did the parents in Nickelodeon's *Drake & Josh* get together?). Even as divorce has become a common occurrence in American society, our culture continues to send us mixed messages.

So, we have come to a time when divorce touches the lives of perhaps half the families in America. Now that civil unions have been legalized in Illinois, the dissolution ("dissolving") of legally recognized personal partnerships will reach new people and populations. With new segments of the population entering into legally binding relationships, we can expect that dissolutions will likewise touch on new families, whatever their form. At the time this volume goes to press, it will be too early to have much experience with the dissolution of the newly created civil unions. The civil union will be discussed briefly later, but it is reasonable to expect that virtually all of our experience with divorce will transfer directly to the dissolution of civil unions. For the purposes of this book, I will include the idea of civil unions when I refer to "marriages," and I will assume that the dissolution of civil unions will be understood when I use the terms "divorce" or "dissolution of marriage."

If, from a legal standpoint, divorce is such a common occurrence, why is there still such ambivalence? This is true probably because there is so much more to divorce than the legal issues. Divorce is a somewhat unique creature that has religious, emotional, financial, and cultural/social components. While your family law attorney cannot practically assist you with all of these aspects, a *good* family law attorney will recognize what effect these issues are having on you and your decisions during the process. A challenge that the good family law attorney must address is giving you legal advice in representing you, while being mindful that these non-legal factors will play a large role in your decision-making and experiences during your divorce.

The purpose of this book, then, is to help introduce the important concepts involved in the Illinois law of divorce, and to help you understand what is involved, the decisions you will have to make, and the steps you will have to take to bring this about. This book is only an introduction to this complex topic, and certainly does not represent a "how to" book.

When meeting with potential clients for an initial consultation, I am often asked about the possibility and advisability of individuals representing themselves in their divorce. I tell prospective clients that Illinois law provides them with the right to represent themselves in all court proceedings. If a litigant chooses to represent himself or herself, however, the court will expect that party to perform with the knowledge, skill, and ability of a veteran family law attorney. In such instances (which refer to litigants representing themselves as *pro se*—Latin for "on their own behalf"), the court *cannot* give help, advice, or "breaks" to the *pro se* litigant. Therefore, I will warn most litigants that representing himself or herself in divorce court is like self-surgery—it's not illegal to remove one's own kidney, it's just a really bad idea. My goal, then, is to introduce the laws and processes of divorce in Illinois to the layperson (non-lawyer) reader, and to help the reader understand and make the important decisions involved in seeking a divorce in Illinois.

1

Initial Considerations

A rose by any other name…

In Illinois law, the legal term for a divorce is "dissolution of marriage"; these terms are interchangeable, although "divorce" is used much more frequently. In 2011, Illinois adopted a law permitting "civil unions." While civil unions end in "dissolution" and not "divorce," for all intents and purposes the two will be interchangeable concepts. Therefore, the discussion in this book relating to divorce should be assumed to apply with equal force to the dissolution of civil unions, unless otherwise noted.

The Many Faces of Divorce

Of all the areas of the law, maybe of all the areas of life experiences, divorce is unique. The termination of marriage has multiple aspects: legal, financial, mental, emotional, and personal. This fact makes a divorce a complex and challenging prospect. While the primary purpose of this book is to introduce you to the legal aspects of a divorce, the other aspects cannot be ignored.

Financial Considerations

Most easily understood is the interplay between the legal and financial aspects of a divorce. There are numerous books and online resources that should be considered to help understand and manage the financial aspects of a divorce. A relatively new concept that has found some acceptance is the "certified divorce planner." A certified divorce planner undertakes a set course of education and certification that leads to being this designation. A certified divorce planner's role is to assist individuals in the divorce process to understand, plan for, and manage the financial impact of a divorce on themselves and their families. Especially in high-income cases, cases where investments are complex, or in cases where family-owned businesses are involved, a certified divorce planner can assist the litigants and their counsel to make sure that the legalities of the divorce take into account the financial realities involved. Of course, consideration has to be given to whether the additional cost of a certified divorce planner is justified, given the parties' assets, cash flow, and what is at stake.

Other useful resources to help assist with the financial impact of divorce include tax preparers, accountants, and financial planners.

One of the most important realizations that the successful litigant will reach is to grasp the vital importance of budget and economic viability. Needless to say, virtually *any* divorce will be an emotional event. Even the most level-headed and mature individual can be distracted by the often competitive nature of a break-up, and the human need to win or feel justified in one's feelings.

In trying to come to terms with a break-up and moving forward into the future, it is entirely understandable and typical for one to become focused on the division of important commodities, such as custody, parenting time and rights, income, assets, and debt. The rough and ready way most people latch onto these divisions is to think of "shares" or "percentages." In setting objectives for trial or settlement, it is quite normal for the parties' thinking to gravitate toward percentages, for example, "I want the kids half of the time" or "I deserve more than half of her income because I put her through school."

A piece of advice that I share with almost every client is something to the effect of "you can't eat percentages." Throughout the process, it is vital for litigants to remember that it is one's budget or cash flow that will have the greatest affect on their ability to survive and enjoy life going forward. As discussed below, I feel that one of—if not *the*—primary objective of a financial settlement needs to be the client's confidence that she will have sufficient access to funds each week to pay for food, clothing, shelter, gasoline, and the other necessities of life. After all, having 75 percent of her husband's pension in twenty years will not "feed the bulldog" today.

Long-term finances are important, too. Beyond the immediate need to pay this month's bills loom the prospects of educating children, future medical expenses, retirement, and the like. Only in the most simple of agreed-upon divorces, both day-to-day and long-term financial considerations are a huge factor that will command much of the attorney's time and attention.

To minimize legal fees, increase the client's sense of confidence and control, and to best ensure the client's satisfaction with the result, it is essential that a divorcing party understand and thoroughly think through his or her financial needs and desires—before and during the divorce process.

The Role of Religion

One's religious beliefs, of course, play a large part in the decision to remain married or to seek a divorce. The Illinois court systems are not well equipped to address the religious aspects of divorce, and therefore, neither are most attorneys. There are certain aspects of religious life, however, that will influence the decisions made by divorcing parties, and so are worthy of brief discussion here. There are, I understand, some religions that forbid adherents from obtaining a divorce. This may have great personal bearing on the parties, but Illinois courts will not consider such religious prohibitions as a defense to a request for a divorce. Likewise, a religious principle that requires the parties to seek counseling or pass some waiting period before seeking a divorce will not be recognized by the Illinois courts.

In a latter chapter, the concept of "legal separation" is discussed (see Chapter 8). In cases where parties are unable to divorce for religious reasons, a legal separation may be appropriate. In a legal separation, the parties remain legally married indefinitely, yet have the legal right to live separate and apart in different residences, and in some cases, have little to no relationship going forward other than being "married" to each other (and therefore being unavailable to marry another or enter into a civil union with anyone else).

Legal custody (which should be distinguished from the related concept of "residential custody") (see Chapter 4) of minor children in Illinois includes the right to make the major religious decisions for the children until they turn eighteen years of age. If the parties agree as to a child's faith and major religious decisions—or if they can cooperate consistently and effectively to make these religious decisions—then joint legal custody may be appropriate. Joint legal custody would, in this example, allow the parties to share equally the major religious decisions for the minors. (This subject is discussed more fully below in Chapter 4.) If the parties cannot cooperate consistently and effectively to decide the child's major religious decisions, then one party or the other will most likely receive sole legal custody of the child.

In some instances, the parties have had disagreements as to religious practices or upbringings throughout the child's life. More frequently, the parties change religious beliefs or a new relationship for one of the adults brings with it new religious faith or practices. Such a change will complicate litigation, as one party will argue that there is an established, "agreed upon" religious pattern for the child, while the other will assert the right to rear the child in his or her new faith.

Another of the three aspects of legal custody is the power to make a minor child's major medical decisions. Certain religions include in their tenets rules relating to medical care for children. If the parties' faiths differ on major medical issues, such as blood transfusions, inoculations, anesthetic, surgery, faith healing, or the like, it would be difficult, if not impossible, for the parties to share legal custody.

The final aspect of legal custody is the power to make the child's major educational decisions. This is another area where religion can play a role. Deciding whether a child attends a public or parochial school, whether a child participates in certain classes or activities, the child's extracurricular activities, and the child's religious education outside of traditional school are all decisions where religion and education may intersect. Further complicating this already difficult area are the financial responsibilities of private schooling. While it is customary to have both parents contribute toward the reasonable and necessary costs of a child's education, courts in most circumstances do not consider private/parochial school "necessary," or the costs of same to be "reasonable."

In some cases, the court will allow one parent (usually, the one with sole legal custody) to choose private school for a child, but will not require the other parent to pay the costs of private school. While courts will sometimes require payment of private school costs (this seems more frequent in Cook County—where private schools are more prevalent) in cases where the child has special needs; or in cases where the parties have long provided private schooling to the child prior to the split, this should not be expected.

Personal, Mental, and Emotional Aspects of Divorce

Clearly, divorce is far more than legal and financial in nature. Divorce lawyers and judges have a fine line to walk in trying to take the personal aspects of divorce into account. I think the biggest challenge facing many who make a living doing this is trying to remember to be sensitive to the novelty of this process to most litigants. After one has done hundreds of divorces, it is important to remember that for most clients, this is their first (hopefully) and only time here. Even if attorneys and judges try to exercise the utmost of sensitivity, it is still a part of their jobs to be objective, if not dispassionate. There are many resources available to litigants to assist them in dealing with the personal and emotional aspects of divorce. Clergy, friends, professional counselors, and shelves full of self-help books are available. Illinois requires the parties to a custody case to attend a parenting class or a seminar that relates to the impact of divorce upon children. This requirement, of course, only applies in cases where children are involved in the divorce. The requirements and contents of these classes differ between the various counties and circuits of the state, but the classes are mandatory. Many of these classes contain advice and identify resources to help parties deal with the impact a divorce has on a family with children.

A popular misconception is that a court can compel parties to attend relationship or marital counseling prior to or during a divorce. While counseling can be ordered in some cases where children's best interests are being affected by the divorce, absent certain factors, a divorce court will not order parties to attend counseling to work on their relationship or to attempt to reconcile. The best advice I can give to people considering or experiencing a divorce is to make sure they recognize and address the personal impact on themselves and their children. I cannot recall an instance where the personal impact on the adult or children was ignored or swept under the rug that did not result in that effect being felt later.

There are really two (if not more) divorces for each divorce case that is filed—the legal/financial divorce, and the emotional divorce. In my twenty-plus years of experience, these two divorces almost *never* occur on the same date. Whether it occurs long before the divorce, during the process, or many years after, the personal/emotional divorce has to be addressed by the parties in any case. In my experience, the inability of one party or the other to reach the "emotional divorce" often leads to the protracted nature of divorce cases. This is true in divorces that are prolonged, because one or the other party is not willing to "let go," or to cases where, even after the divorce is finalized, parties keep coming back to court again and again to litigate issues.

Many parents are acutely aware of the emotional and real life impact of a divorce on their children. I have seen parents address this impact with a wide variety of care, sensitivity, and effectiveness. To the parent who wishes to help their children through this process and wishes to manage the impact to the children to the very best extent possible, I echo the preflight instructions from your flight attendant:

> In the event things go wrong, take care of yourself—if you cannot make sure the oxygen mask is securely on your face, you may not be able to help others.

How Can I Help You?—Understanding the Limitations of the Legal System

Early on in my practice as a family law attorney, I reprogrammed myself to avoid the typical greeting: "Hi, how are you?" I had quickly learned that my prospective clients were not doing well, or they would not be in to see me. I gave thought to my purpose in being there, as well as why the client had come in to see me, and changed my standard greeting in almost every case to: "How can I help you?"

As a final consideration, the prospective litigant needs to know what the court can and cannot do.

Like any game or competition, divorce is governed by a set of rules—a lengthy set of rules. The written rules controlling Illinois law can be found in the Illinois Marriage and Dissolution of Marriage Act[1], and following. Throughout the book, I reference some, but not all, of the relevant Illinois laws that you will encounter in this process. The court can sometimes use its discretion in making decisions, and the court must sometimes interpret the rules. But, by and large, the court is limited by the contents of those rules. Although few clients do so, it seems that more parties to divorce are reading and trying to understand these rules. Understanding the rules, or more importantly, understanding that these rules *control* your divorce and much of its outcome, is vital to your experience. Our notions of "fairness," and the silliness of reality as presented on court television shows, color most of our beliefs about how court will or should work. Certainly, the law includes an understanding of fairness, and I believe that virtually all of our judges try to be "fair." But the idea of "fairness" is greatly misunderstood and overemphasized when the courthouse door is crossed.

While fairness with justice is the aim of the process, one should be aware that "fair" is not a universal or indisputable idea. Usually, both parties, even when they are far apart, feel that their position is "fair." For this reason alone, do not get too hung up on the idea of seeking or receiving what is "fair." You may read the top of the box for the game of LIFE, or

---

[1] 750 ILCS §§ 5/101-5/802 (West 2012).

football's rules for pass interference, and feel that they are "unfair." But in both games, what is written in the rules will control—not someone's idea of justice or equity. Thus, an important day in the litigant's process is when he or she comes to understand that so much of what is to come is foretold—it is in the written rules of Illinois divorce law that most of the future is to be decided. While each case is different, while there is room for negotiation, and while your attorney can and should present evidence that will help the judge apply the rules and exercise his or her discretion in your favor, the point is that your time in court is not Judge Judy, or story time. In fact, the judge's determination will not be governed by his or her understanding of what you or your spouse believes to be fair. The rules and procedures discussed below will govern your divorce, and comprehending that should help bring you understanding and peace of mind during and after this process.

2

Go In with a Plan

There are many benefits to approaching your divorce with a well thought out plan in place. Time and effort put into a plan will pay off many times over. Having a plan will improve your experience by helping to limit surprises; streamlining later efforts by you and your attorney; lessening the stress on you and your children (if any); and perhaps, most importantly, giving you a much-needed feeling of security and control in a time of upheaval and uncertainty.

Much of this advice will seem intuitive, if not overly obvious. My experience has shown, however, that only a very small percentage of divorce clients put sufficient time and effort into planning and preparing for a divorce. Those who do, I believe, not only get better results, but also have a much higher level of satisfaction with the process. One point I try to emphasize with clients is the importance of their *experience*. Divorce, like any sort of litigation, is a highly uncertain endeavor. Even the most experienced attorney with an excellent grasp of the facts of your case will have a limited ability to predict the outcome of your case. Many times, even clients with the strongest cases and the best representation come away with certain dissatisfactions and disappointments. It is often said that, "No one wins in a divorce," and even a litigant who emerges having "won" every aspect of a case can come away bloodied, bruised, and thousands of dollars lighter.

Because even the "best" divorces are still difficult and emotional, I believe that great effort should be placed on trying to make the "experience" of the divorce as comfortable, or at least tolerable, as possible. Even the best attorneys have limited control over the *results* of your case—but a good and aware attorney can work with the client to maximize the client's journey.

Step 1: Set Goals

The first step to formulating your plan is to define your goals. The first step in any journey is to define where one wishes to go. A party seeking to dissolve a marriage would seem to have one simple goal—to end the relationship. Naturally, this goal is usually primary in the mind of the client. For this reason, the client will often overemphasize the "whys and wherefores" of the relationship in the initial meetings with the attorney. As discussed later, the reasons for the break-up and failure of the marriage have very little legal significance. In outlining your plan, the psychological benefits of reflecting on the failures of the relationship are necessary and beneficial—but this topic should not occupy much of your effort in planning for the divorce.

At least where children are involved, the party seeking the divorce should assess what their hope is for managing the impact of the divorce on the children. An important consideration is deciding what your desire is in terms of the children's relationship with your former spouse. Whether your personal goal for the divorce with regard to your ex-spouse ranges from being friends, to focusing on being effective partners in parenting, to no contact with him or her ever again, this goal will need to be filtered through an honest assessment of the needs of the children involved. I often tell clients that, in a real sense, they remain "married" to their spouse until their children graduate from college (if not longer!). A big step in goal setting, then, is three decisions regarding your future:

1. What future relationship do you want with your ex;
2. What kind of "divorce" do you want your children to have; and
3. What kind of parenting relationship do you hope to create in the future?

The next tier of decisions relate to your wishes for the next phase of your life. Your litigation strategy should be fashioned with the aim of helping you achieve your goals for the future. A primary concern for most litigants is their future economic viability. You will need to consider how you will provide for yourself and others during this divorce, in the short term afterwards, and for the rest of your life. The first two phases are often overlooked, as the bright future of "happily ever after" is a natural focus to get you through the difficult times. As discussed below, while often uncertain, the issue of economics during the divorce is crucial. Naturally, you will have to have shelter, food, and be able to pay the bills while the divorce is in progress. If you are not able to be economically viable during the divorce, you run the risk of not being able to "go the distance." Failure to plan for your expenses during the divorce can result in your inability to pay counsel, your need to acquire additional debt, loss of assets, damage to your credit, and a very real strategic disadvantage. If you cannot afford to have your attorney complete your case, you may face the significant disadvantage of changing counsel midstream, or trying to represent yourself against a knowledgeable, experienced, and trained family law attorney. This situation is often referred to as "taking a knife to a gun fight."

Even if your attorney stays with your case during your "cash crunch," your strategic position can be significantly compromised by a failure in short-term planning. If you have not adequately planned for your finances during the case, you may need to concede on certain issues or "settle short" over all because you are being "starved out." A not-uncommon strategy is to try to grind your opponent down using a "war of attrition." One party will dig in, cut off access to cash flow or assets, and try to starve the other out. Lack of planning plays into this strategy perfectly. If the party with better access to cash flow (or a better plan) can wait the other out, the latter party may have to settle some issues, or the entire case, on unfavorable terms.

I think this strategy is especially dangerous now that recent changes in Illinois law require that custody issues be given priority and resolved first. The party trying to use this "siege" strategy may be able to gain concessions from you in the custody aspects of the case, if you do not have the financial ability to withstand a prolonged battle.

A final complicating factor is the uncertainty about how long the litigation will last. I once took a divorce all the way from initial filing to finalization in about a month, but that was a very unusual situation (wherein both parties were very anxious to get out of the country). On the other end of the extreme are the prolonged custody fights that can take five years or more. Most cases fall somewhere in the middle, with three to six months being a quick case, and six to twelve months representing a more typical duration. An important early question for you and your attorney should be how long your case might reasonably be expected to last. Be hesitant to accept any hard and fast answers or guarantees, but try to get a range of possible durations to help you plan financially.

An often-overlooked aspect of planning is an approach to the months following the divorce. In many jurisdictions, litigants are expected to complete an exchange of financial statements that spells out each party's *current* knowledge as to income, expenses, assets, debts, and other pertinent financial data. Each party fills one of these disclosures out on their own; it is not intended to be a "group project." This can be a difficult and sometimes daunting task for many. Quite a few people are dependent on their spouse for their day-to-day financial affairs, and they often have no idea as to their finances. Completing a form like this is an important tool that will help you organize your thoughts in so many ways. It is an invaluable asset to your attorney, for assessing your current needs, as well as in trying to project your needs into the future. An accurate financial statement can help you understand your financial situation now, and what you need in the future. It will also help you learn about financial information known to your spouse, of which you might be unaware. I find this exchange can be a very important step for helping clients set their expectations—or to help the opponent have a more realistic set of expectations, after all the cards are on the table.

I have included one such statement (see Appendix C). It is the Comprehensive Financial Statement (CFS) currently used in Kane and Kendall counties of Illinois. Your court may use a different format, but it is probably similar enough. You may want to fill out this form *now* just to see where you are, and how much you know or do not know about your financial life.

Although your lawyer may have a different form, or some particular preference or tips for filling out such a disclosure, it is recommended that you fill out such a form prior to meeting your attorney. Doing so will help you better understand your position, and communicate it to your attorney. As your case progresses, your financial disclosure will be updated, or modified, as your finances will inevitably change because of the process. Completing, revising, and using your CFS throughout the process is a good way to understand where you are, and to help you plan for where you wish to go.

While your financial disclosures are intended to provide a snapshot of your present circumstances, they can be helpful to aid even looking at your short- and long-term goals. Using multiple copies and filling them out can help you plan possible budgets, income needs, and financial structures for your future.

Step 2: Identify Your Resources

Once your goals are set, you will need to assess the resources you have, and the resources you will need, to reach your objectives.

Decide what you will need to get where you want to go. At first, the list may seem overwhelming. Try to think in all three phases: what you need to get through the divorce; what you will need for life in the short term after the divorce; and what you will need to have for the future you wish. It may help to think of this list as a packing list, or a collection of tools that you will need.

Included as Appendix A is a sample checklist to use or that might give you ideas to start your own list of resources.

Creating a list like this may be intimidating at first, as you come to realize all that is needed, and what you may lack. But it may also be encouraging, when you realize the resources already at your disposal. It can also be calming, if the list itself becomes a resource, as you utilize it to go about getting the tools you will need. Like most things in the divorce process, this list can morph and change as your situation evolves.

Step 3: Assemble Your Team

Now that you have goals, and have identified what resources you have and what you will need, it is time to put together your team. You will be guided by the needs you have identified and the resources you have at hand. Deciding who to include in your divorce team, and how deeply to involve each party, is an important and personal choice. Many of my clients have a friend/family member (or so) who acts as a primary confidant, sounding board, or "buddy." This "helper" will often accompany my client to the initial interviews, or to further meetings. Whether a third party joins in our meetings is entirely up to the client. The client is always warned, however, that the presence of the third party has an important impact on the idea of confidentiality. Clients are advised that virtually anything they tell us in secret is held in the strictest of confidence. With a few exceptions (such as a client confiding that they intend to commit a serious crime or harm another individual), an attorney cannot communicate confidential information received from a client—not even to the judge. A communication is confidential, however, *only* if it is made in secret. This means that anything a client tells an attorney in the presence of any third party is *not* a secret—and is therefore not strictly protected by the attorney/client privilege. Of course, an attorney should always do his or her best to keep a client's secret, no matter where or how it is communicated. A client's secrets could be subject to discovery if not communicated in private, so I always warn clients of this fact. I tell them that if there is any aspect of their case for which they wish to ensure there is a true attorney/client protected "privilege" secret, it must be told to me outside the presence of any third party—even if the third party knows the secret (or *is* the secret).

This is the point at which the client needs to decide if and who they will retain as their attorney. I suppose this topic alone could take several chapters, but that is not the intention of this book. There are many ways to find an attorney, or a pool of attorneys from which to choose. In previous times, most people found an attorney in the yellow pages, or by asking friends and acquaintances. Marketing experts tell us that telephone books are a thing of past, but in most communities, you will still find many attorneys listed in the phone books. You will also encounter a variety of listings or advertisements for family law attorneys, both in the phone books and in other print ads.

Attorneys and their ability to advertise are heavily regulated in Illinois, and most other jurisdictions. Among the many rules governing advertising lawyers' services in Illinois are prohibitions from dishonest or misleading advertising, implying that an attorney is "certified" or "specializes" in family law (because no such certification or specializations exist in Illinois family law), or implying or guaranteeing results.

Another popular way of finding an attorney whom you might be interested in hiring is by obtaining personal recommendations from others. Because divorce touches so many lives, you probably know several people who have been through, or are currently going through, a divorce. Their direct personal experience with local attorneys could be very helpful in guiding your thoughts in choosing an attorney. Not only can friends and family provide insight into particular attorneys, discussing the experience with others will certainly help you get an idea as to what is involved in working with an attorney, and what type of attorney you might be looking for stylistically. Of course, how someone feels about an attorney they used, or went up against, should probably be viewed like a movie review or dining review, in that everyone's personal taste varies. "War stories" from others should give you good insight into available attorneys in your area.

Other attorneys can also help you find a good family law attorney. In our increasingly complicated legal world, the idea of the "general practitioner" attorney is fast becoming obsolete. Law is an area where the phrase "jack of all trades, master of none" surely applies. It is virtually impossible for any lawyer to be competent in all areas of the law, let alone good or better in every area. I often ask prospective clients to whom they would go for heart surgery: a cardiologist or a general practitioner? The area of family law is complex and ever evolving, and this area represents a full-time vocation. I have chosen to focus on family law as my career—and so I do not do real estate closings, incorporate business, or try personal injury cases. Even if a client very much wants me to represent them in an area outside my expertise, I will refer them to an attorney I know who focuses their practice in the relevant field. Beware the "general practitioner" who says he can do your bankruptcy, defend your murder trial, do your business merger with Apple, and litigate your custody case. If you know a good attorney whom you trust, he should be a good resource in directing you to a qualified attorney in family law.

Other professionals can be an excellent source for referrals to attorneys in divorce law. Attorneys in other fields, accountants, tax preparers, counselors, psychiatrists, or doctors, and other professionals have frequent contact with family law attorneys, and may be able to suggest an attorney who will be a good fit for you.

Most counties in Illinois have bar associations. In smaller communities, where multiple counties are organized into what are called judicial circuits, there are usually bar associations of some sort. If you look up the bar association for the county or circuit where you live, they will most likely have a referral service, or a list of local practitioners who focus on family law.

Attorneys are not required to belong to bar associations; they only need to be admitted to the bar (law school graduates who have passed the state bar exam, and met certain background and personal investigations), and be registered with the state each year. When considering any attorney, prospective clients should always log onto www.ardc.org. This is the website for the Illinois Supreme Court Attorney Registration and Disciplinary Commission, which is the governing body for all attorneys in Illinois. Once on this website, you can enter an attorney's name and make sure they are licensed, and not subject to investigation or other disciplinary action.

While registration is the only mandatory requirement, bar association membership is a valuable qualification in assessing a prospective attorney. An attorney who is a member of a bar association is generally better known to other attorneys and judges, is more likely to be involved in the activity and administration of the local legal community, and often more likely to be involved in continuing legal education, community service, and other activities that improve an attorney's knowledge, skill, and effectiveness. Through the local bar association, you can find out which attorneys are more active in things like continuing education, presentations, and education for other attorneys and the public, and things like writing articles on the law. Many bar associations also have lawyer referral services, or lists of local attorneys who focus their practice on family law.

Of course, the new and growing place to find your friendly neighborhood divorce lawyer is the Internet. Even just a few years ago, I had no idea I would be "Googled" by so many potential clients. Marketing professionals, and people trying to sell us listings on marketing websites, tell us that this is where most people will find their attorneys in the future. Obviously, many will use search engines or web browsers to search for local attorneys using search terms such as the name of their community and "divorce attorney" or "family law." Many websites also collect and provide listings of attorneys, such as lawyers.com, lawyerpages.com, and divorce.com. These websites focus on providing information about family law and local practitioners in that area. From either of these sources, you will most likely reach a number of individual attorney or law firm websites.

The Internet will provide you with a dazzling, maybe overwhelming, assortment of information and attorneys. I think the best advice here, as anywhere, is to be an informed consumer. Evaluate the data that the Internet provides to decide if it is accurate and trustworthy. I am a little leery of "review" sites, which purport to allow clients to post reviews for attorneys or law firms. These reviews are anonymous in most cases, and should be evaluated like any anonymous statement on the Internet. Be aware that the person "reviewing" an attorney or firm may have never used that attorney or firm, may be the bitter ex-spouse of someone the attorney represented, or may be a former client who has an "ax to grind," that has nothing to do with the quality of the attorney's representation. These review sites sometimes contain valuable reviews and information, and sometimes are suspect. I think these may be part of your search, but probably cannot replace personal recommendations or a review from someone actually known to you.

Once you have found one or more attorneys that you believe could do a good job representing you, you should choose one or more to interview. I know many clients start with a list of about three attorneys that they want to interview or investigate further. I do not think there is any replacement for a face-to-face meeting to interview and ask questions of your prospective attorney.

If distance or other circumstances prohibit you from meeting face-to-face, a lengthy telephone interview with the attorney is a must. In larger firms, there are senior, more experienced attorneys, who are referred to most often as "partners." They are often the best known, most skilled, and most in demand attorneys at the firm. Newer or less experienced attorneys are commonly referred to as "associates."

If your research leads you to want one of the firm's partners as your attorney, you will want to find out how the firm distributes work and responsibility between partners and associates. In larger firms, you may retain the partner or firm, but much of the work and face-to-face contact may be with an associate. If this suits you, this arrangement is fine, so long as it meets your expectations. The important thing is to determine whether you want the partner only to work on your case and interact with you, or if you are comfortable with the partner supervising your case, and some portion of your representation being handled by associates, paralegals, or other members of the firm. Keep in mind that partners and associates often bill you at different rates.

Before selecting your attorney or firm, I think you should know who will be handling what parts of your case, and have a face-to-face meeting with the attorney who will be supervising your case and who will be primarily responsible for your case and for direct contact with you.

I tell clients who are looking for a family law attorney that I believe there are three crucial elements they should look for:

1. An attorney who focuses their practice on family law, and who is qualified to handle their case;
2. An attorney who will communicate with them and whose communication style matches theirs; and

3. An attorney they trust and feel they will have a good working relationship with.

As discussed above, family law is a complex and constantly changing area that requires an attorney to devote great time and effort to mastering and staying the best in the field. If an attorney does not focus all or a very substantial portion of his or her time on divorce work, he or she will not be known and trusted by the judges and other attorneys in the family law area. Having a family law attorney whom the judges and opposing counsel know and trust can be a valuable asset, and can increase your chances of success and minimize your delays and expenses. Of course, you will also want an attorney who knows the law, the recent changes to the law, and is aware of new cases or developments in the law and practice.

Your attorney should be qualified to handle your sort of case. A newer, less experienced attorney may be fine for your child support case, or to represent you in a simple divorce. They may not be a good choice, however, to take your case to trial or to lead you through a very prolonged custody battle. Even among attorneys who do family law full time, you will find a wide variety of experience and skills. Some attorneys will pride themselves on the number of cases they have tried, while others will emphasize their success at settling cases and avoiding trial. Some very qualified family law attorneys relish custody trials, while others will not take cases if custody is truly an issue. Even very well regarded attorneys will have varying comfort levels with the issues like hotly contested or "ugly" cases, custody disputes, high dollar or financially complex cases, or cases that present new divorces as opposed to post-divorce litigation. Ask many questions, and listen closely to the answers to learn your prospective attorney's qualifications, comfort zones, and expertise before you choose who will be your advocate.

I can think of no element more key to your satisfaction with your representation than your attorney's ability to communicate. Your attorney's skill and knowledge will not mean much to you if you do not understand what is being done. You are not likely to understand or be comfortable with the divorce process if your attorney cannot or will not communicate with you. It is also unlikely for you to be able to make an informed decision or be satisfied with the results if you are not communicated with well. Therefore, it is important to determine if your attorney will communicate with you sufficiently, and whether you communicate well with the attorney. Some of this is a matter of the speed and frequency with which your attorney communicates with you. Will he give you advance notice of deadlines, court dates, and important events? Will she advise you after court or other important events as to what has happened? Will your attorney answer questions? Will he or she ask questions to make sure they understand you and your wishes? Each case and client merits a different level of communication, but it is important to make sure that *you* are content with the attorney's willingness and ability to communicate with you. Then, keep in mind that good communication is a two-way street. For you to work as a team, your attorney must communicate with you as quickly and as often as you wish. Equally, attorneys must be willing and able to listen to you. Make sure your information needs and desires match what your attorney can and will do to communicate with you.

Lastly, there is the very subjective issue of communication style. There are persons who are intelligent, organized, and capable communicators whose interpersonal style is not well suited to other, equally capable individuals. No matter how well I try to talk and listen, I cannot seem to reach or understand some clients. Whether it is because of their language or cultural difference, or just a fundamental difference as to how we communicate, some clients are not a good match for some attorneys, communication-wise. Use a personal interview to try to determine if your attorney—wordy or brief, eloquent or blunt, warm and engaging, or hard and cool—is someone with whom you can communicate well.

Finally, it is important that there be a "good fit" and level of trust between you and your counsel. This is not to say that you should be interviewing for a lifelong friend, or someone that you even necessarily "like." What you should be looking for is *trust* and *belief* on some level—you need to believe in your advocate, and trust that he or she is working hard and looking out for your best interests. Regardless of how an issue is resolved, you should finish feeling that you were given your best chance of success and that you were thoroughly represented. I find that clients who are most satisfied, win or lose, are those who have been communicated with, felt a part of the team, and trusted that they were being treated with honesty by an attorney who was doing a good job and working hard for them.

Your Expectations and Things to Look for in Your Advocate

In my experience, clients are most impressed by promptness and responsiveness. I think many clients come into the attorney/client relationship, especially in complex family matters, expecting lengthy delay and a certain lack of accessibility to their attorney and their case. My focus, from initial telephone or in person contact with the client, through completion of the case, is on *listening*. Rather than trying to impress a client with my knowledge of the law, the local courts, and old "war stories" regarding successes in court, I prefer to initially let clients do the vast majority of the talking. I believe that most clients, first and foremost, want to tell their story. I believe if attorneys listen attentively to your story—even (or especially) to the parts that are not legally relevant but are personally relevant to you—trust, communication, and a good bond are formed. For this reason, my initial client questionnaire is not too law-intensive. Rather, I do have the client fill out a basic questionnaire, but I gather much of the information through the initial interviews with the clients and by taking notes.

Any attorney who is organized, efficient, and manages your case well is likely to get a good result and be more cost-efficient for you. I have an established protocol for each type of case. For example, in a divorce involving children, I have a packet of documents, a self-created timeline, and a protocol that I almost invariably follow. I believe the litigator is able to provide better creative thinking and more unique approaches to the individual client when he is not distracted by procedure, details, or the more mundane "cookie cutter" issues that are part of every case. To the extent that one can streamline and standardize the initial approach to a case, I believe the better one can provide personalized and creative service to the client.

Many clients are looking for a particular type of personality that meets their needs in their case. Some clients are looking for a "hand holder" attorney, some are looking for a "bull dog," some seek a "strategist," and many clients seek someone they will view as a "protector." Early on, the client needs to understand that different approaches to a case (extensive discovery and fighting each and every issue versus a more cooperative approach to the case) will yield different case durations, different budgets, and different relationships post-decree with former spouses and even the children. The initial interview is your opportunity to determine the attorney's particular personality, and decide whether your client's style and approach is well suited to your needs and situation.

After a client has signed the contract and paid the retainer, I follow up immediately with a fairly lengthy engagement letter (see LSA, Appendix F). An engagement letter is essential for setting the tone of the relationship, how your attorney will represent you, and the ordinary business practices of your office. I find that many of the client's FAQs can be addressed, in advance, with a solid retainer letter.

Most attorneys use an entry letter or conversation to explain the court's required parenting class. In such a letter, I explain the program, the necessary requirements and timeline, and the benefits to the client and the children that can accrue from attending the class promptly and with an open mind (Appendix F). This is also a good opportunity to introduce clients to a new factor in their life and decision making that is represented by the power of the court. In many cases, this is the first time where someone outside the family circle will make a decision or issue a mandate regarding you and your spouse.

Consistent with my comments above, I have clients begin working on their Comprehensive Financial Statement (Appendix C) as quickly as possible. I explain to the clients that this is usually a mandatory procedure, and that completing it promptly will reflect well on them in court. I go on to explain that if both parties promptly exchange a complete and appropriately documented Comprehensive Financial Statement, an open exchange of information—if not a dialog or trust—can be created. If both sides are willing to "show their cards" promptly and fairly, not only will the financial and legal divorce proceed more efficiently, but also it may assist the clients in reaching the "emotional divorce."

It is frequently said that clients in a divorce case enter the office unhappy, and regardless of the result, they probably will leave unhappy. Even in the case of a "good" divorce, this is still an upsetting, life-changing, and most likely expensive, event in the life of the parties. As virtually every client has said to me, "I never expected to be here." It is important that each client understand that the results of the case, while they can certainly be affected by your skill and advocacy, are ultimately determined by the laws and the judge. While we all want our clients to feel that they have succeeded or obtained their objectives, we know that this is not always possible. My measure of success in the representation of my client is, at the end of the case, to be certain that my client has been fully informed throughout the process; has taken part in and felt a part of the process; and comes away with a clear understanding of *what* occurred and *why* the result was reached. Frequent communication with the client, and responsiveness to the client's needs, are the keystones to success in such an approach.

Gathering Information and Preparing to Succeed

The steps you may take in the early stages of your divorce may vary, based on your attorney's advice or wishes. Following are some ideas for preparations you may want to make before your divorce case is initiated, along with some information you should gather.

Protect Yourself

It should go without saying that the most important thing in your divorce is you and your children, if you have any. Accordingly, you need to protect yourself and your safety—first and foremost.

If there has been a history of abuse or violence, or if my client feels that the filing of the divorce may lead to abuse or violence, I suggest that they have an emergency plan and a "bug out bag" in place. There is no legal consideration or strategy that is more important than your safety, so leaving the house, if only temporarily, may be a necessity. If a client is concerned about abuse or violence, I ask my client to have an escape plan in place. Factors to take into account are:

- Having money or a credit card available;
- Securing transportation;
- Arranging for a safe place to stay;

- Making sure they have a cell phone or other method of communication;
- Making plans for getting their children to and from school, continuing their work obligations, and other day-to-day necessities; and
- Packing an emergency "bug out bag" with a change of clothes, medications, and other short-term necessities.

Long-term preparations focus on the gathering of information. Although the discovery process discussed in Chapter 7 should lead to a full disclosure of all of the financial information of the parties, this process can take a long time. There are also instances where the opposing party deliberately hides or destroys information. Lastly, information can be lost, deleted, or destroyed accidentally or on purpose, with the passage of time, and in particular with the dependence on computers and electronic storage.

For these reasons, you may want to gather as much financial information as you can as early as possible. Gathering data may:

1. Help you and your attorney assess the case;
2. Help you and your attorney decide on strategy;
3. Allow you to fill in gaps and discovery from your opponent;
4. Help you complete your discovery responses; and
5. Make life easier during the litigation process.

Information you should consider gathering and keeping safe as early as possible includes:

- Check stubs
- W-2s
- Tax returns
- Bank statements
- Retirement account statements
- Mortgage information and statements
- Utility bills
- Credit card statements

- Account passwords and
- Monthly bills, budgets, and other financial information

Retaining Your Attorney

Once you have chosen your attorney, he or she needs to be formally retained. In Illinois, a written contract is strongly preferred. An attorney's ability to enforce this contract and seek an award of fees against you at the end of the attorney's work is limited if a written contract is absent. If your attorney does not require you to sign a written contract, it is probably a cause for concern. The contract should spell out what the attorney has been retained to do, the rate to be charged (usually by the hour, see below), and the amount of the retainer. Any written contract for divorce work should include a written statement of the client's rights and responsibilities, (see Appendix D). This form has been developed by the Illinois Supreme Court and the Attorney Registration and Disciplinary Commission, and should be a part of your contract. If this form is not incorporated into your contract, your attorney's ability to use the divorce law to get a judgment against you for fees is sharply limited. Your attorney can still use ordinary contract law to enforce any obligation to him or her, but the divorce procedure relating to fees does not apply. Ideally, the written contract between you and your attorney will spell out more fully the details of their services to you and how the two of you will interact. Attached is a sample of the base contract used by my office, (Appendix E) along with a follow-up Legal Services Agreement, (Appendix F) which more fully details how I represent my clients.

There are a variety of ways that attorneys are paid to represent you and your case. Some of the financial details of your relationship with your attorney are subject to negotiation between you and your attorney, while others are governed by Illinois law.

In most cases, divorce lawyers in Illinois charge for their services by the hour. This approach was almost universal prior to the last ten years or so, although "flat fees" (as discussed below) were also sometimes used. In an hourly fee case, the attorney's services are charged on an hour-by-hour basis, with the attorney keeping track of time on some agreed upon interval. Quarter-hour intervals are customary, although some attorneys charge by the tenth of the hour. This choice may be negotiable in some offices, but some attorneys' offices, bookkeeping, and billing systems may not accommodate certain increments, and they may be unwilling or unable to negotiate this detail. I do not think there is a significant difference to the client—so long as the attorney's billing practices are honest and consistent.

When charged by the billable hour, your attorneys should provide you with detailed invoices on a regular interval. Although some attorneys send invoices/statements on an irregular basis, or at the end of the case, I do not think this is a good idea for the attorney, or especially for the client. There are many advantages to regular billing statements during the case. Regular statements show the client how much they are spending. This keeps the economic reality of the case before the client, and prevents unpleasant surprises at the end of the case. A client can better judge his ability to afford future litigation if they regularly see how much they are spending. A regular, detailed bill will also let the clients see the direct costs of their litigation choices. Sometimes, a client will want a very aggressive, "no holds barred" approach, until the end of the first month when they see how much this is going to cost. Detailed statements should also tell the client exactly what is going on in their case. We send a detailed statement twice a month, and the time entries are a good status report to the client. A copy of such a statement is attached at the end of this book (Appendix J). Each time entry tells what was done ("telephone call to"), who was involved ("to attorney for the wife"), why it was done ("to discuss failure to pay child support"), when it was done (each entry is dated), and how much was charged (.25 hours). Keeping such detailed entries allows the client to read each interval's statement, and give the client a blow-by-blow description of everything that was done for them during that time.

Although our contract makes it clear that the client is to be charged for everything we do on their behalf, there are times that I will perform a task for free. Even when I choose not to charge for a task, I still "bill" the time, and show it as a "no charge." By doing so, I can keep track of what was done and when. At some later date, I (or my client) can review the bill and see that I tried to call opposing counsel (again), even though they failed to return my call (again). It also tends to make my client happy to see that I am working on their behalf, *and* not charging.

I do not think it is acceptable for an attorney charging by the hour to not keep track of each time entry, to not make their time descriptions adequate for the client to tell exactly what was done with the time, or to not send bills until the end of a case. Doing so does not encourage trust by the client, or communicate very well with the client (violating two of my three rules expressed above).

There are two major philosophies regarding the billable hour. Some attorneys charge the same amount for all tasks, while others have a different rate for work performed at different times (such as in or out of court). Some attorneys charge a different rate for traveling to and from court, as compared to their regular billing rate.

Both of these approaches can be fair and legitimate, depending on whether the attorney bills for time consistently and fairly. I personally do not believe in charging different rates for in- and out-of-court work. I feel that doing so tends to devalue out-of-court work, which can be as or more important than time spent in court. I also feel that it overvalues time in court in some cases. While time spent in court is, indeed, some of the most demanding, many court dates are continuances, or minutes (or hours) of waiting before anything happens. I also do not feel like a discounted rate needs to be charged for travel to and from court, because time spent in transit is just as valuable as any other time during the day, and it is time that I cannot spend on any other matters or clients. To ensure that travel time is billed fairly, however, I divide drive time equally between each client for whom I am appearing in court on that date.

Later on, I will discuss new developments in approach to billing attorney time in family law cases. One such concept that is coming to increasing acceptance is the idea of "block billing." When block billing is used, attorneys and clients agree, at the beginning of a case, that there are certain tasks that will be billed a certain minimum amount of time. Attorneys and clients will sometimes agree that the preparation of pleadings or court appearances will always be billed at a certain minimal amounts, such as a minimum of one hour per task. It is important to note that, if an attorney chooses to use "block billing" or minimum billing for tasks, that this policy should be agreed to in advance by the client, and should be spelled out clearly in the attorney/client contract. I personally believe that this practice is legitimate and often encourages efficiency and value for the client, but I would have concerns employing this practice without telling the client about it and receiving their consent in advance.

Most clients, of course, are concerned about the hourly rate they are being charged for the billable hour. There is no standard, or "right" amount that you should be charged, as a reasonable hourly rate will vary across time, community, and type of case. Some attorneys charge one rate per billable hour for all work that they perform, reasoning that one hour of their time is always worth the same dollar amount. Others charge different hourly rates, based on the type and difficulty of the work presented, reasoning that one hour spent calculating child support is not as taxing as one hour spent cross-examining the opponent during a custody trial. While I generally have a "going rate" for the time and jurisdiction involved, I have been known to discount that rate if I feel that the work is very straightforward, or the client has a worthwhile case and my usual hourly rate is beyond his or her means.

As part of your interview process, you should be asking questions about the hourly rate and how it is applied. After speaking with two or three attorneys, you may have an idea as to what "market" rate is for a case of your type in your community.

That said, however, you should expect some variation in the hourly rates you are quoted. Even for the very same case in the same jurisdiction, attorneys may legitimately quote different hourly rates or financial arrangements. The most obvious reason to differ in hourly rates is the experience and expertise of the attorneys involved. In considering hourly rates of attorneys, think of your experience at the car rental at an airport. While the distance and trip stay the same, your experience is likely to be different if you rent "basic" transportation or the largest luxury model available on the lot. The amount an attorney charges per hour is affected by numerous variables, such as the size and location of their offices, the level of technology and resources they apply in their work, and their level of staffing. You are likely to receive a different level of service and experience from a large law firm that employs secretaries, associates, and paralegals who can assist your attorney, as opposed to a sole practitioner whose office staff may consist of an answering machine. Like most of the decisions you will make, there is no right answer to this question. You will need to decide what level of experience, expertise, reputation, and service you expect from your attorney, as well as what level of representation you will need based upon the type of your case. The needs of your case (simple or difficult), your expectations (a newer attorney or one who offers more basic services versus one of the more experienced attorneys in town with a full service firm), and your budget will help you decide whether the hourly rate and services quoted to you are appropriate for your wishes.

In more than twenty years of practice, I have, of course, encountered an increasing number of clients who need to be very budget conscious, based on the current economic conditions. I have also dealt with more than a few "shoppers," who are absolutely obsessed with the hourly rate charged, who seem much more interested in playing hardball negotiator with me than with having me represent them in their case. I have found, however, that the vast majority of the clients I have served over the years have not been especially concerned about the hourly rate, if they feel that we have a good rapport, that they trust me, and they feel we have done a good job on their case. Divorce clients are already placing such a great deal of trust and reliance in their attorneys, that I often find that the issue of hourly rate is not a great one. If someone is willing to entrust their future and the future of their children to me, more often than not, they expect that I will treat them fair when it comes to the bill.

For many years, a "retainer" referred to a sum that a client paid to have an attorney available, pretty much at any time the client needed. Essentially, the attorney did not perform any services in return for this type of retainer—the attorney was paid to be "available" to the client. This sort of retainer is seldom, if ever, used anymore in Illinois.

Under current practice in Illinois, at least in the area of family law, a retainer is a deposit of funds in the attorney's trust account, to be earned by the attorney in working on the case. Attorneys require a retainer to be paid up front, so that things like filing fees and other customary out-of-pocket expenses are covered and do not come out of the attorney's own pocket. In fact, it is unethical for an attorney to advance things like the filing fee required by the court from out of their own pocket. A considerable amount of work is often needed at the beginning of a divorce case, and an attorney wants to make sure that they are paid for the up-front work that is done. So, in addition to paying for the out-of-pocket expenses relating to a case (called "costs," "court costs," or "expenses"), the retainer is also used to pay attorney's fees that are billed. This is where the importance of the periodic statements comes in. Even when the client does not "owe" the attorney because there are sufficient funds on retainer, a statement should be generated to show amounts and for what reason time was billed, and how much of the retainer is being used for the given period.

Except in limited circumstances, such as flat fees or bundled/component billing cases, such as discussed below, retainers in Illinois divorces *must* be refundable. If an attorney finishes working for a client before the retainer is exhausted, because the client or the attorney wishes to terminate representation, or the case is completed, then the attorney is required to refund the portion of the retainer that has not been properly billed and earned. Make sure that your contract provides that any unearned retainer is to be refunded to you—a "non-refundable" retainer is unethical and not permitted (except as noted below).

The amount of the retainer is also an important consideration for most clients. Clients are often anxious to start their case, but may have trouble getting the amount required by the attorney for a retainer. A careful balance needs to be struck, for the benefit of both the client and the attorney. A smaller retainer is easier for the client to afford or gather. The problem with a small retainer, however, is that they run out much faster. The difficulty, complexity, anticipated length, and the assets available in your case will all affect your attorney's willingness and ability to work once the retainer is exhausted. Before the recent real estate collapse, attorneys were generally more comfortable proceeding once the retainer was exhausted. When most clients had houses with a considerable amount of equity, or where home equity loans/refinances were readily available, there was much less risk in working on a case where the retainer was exhausted. In the pre-2008 economy, an attorney could usually be assured that they would be promptly paid out of the equity in the marital home. Similarly, retirement accounts such as 401(k)s and the like also represented a method for attorneys to be easily paid if they worked through the case and the retainer had been exhausted. With many client's homes upside down (worth less than is owed), this traditional source of attorneys' fees has largely dried up. Even where there is equity in homes, the real estate market has still conspired to make it hard to pay your attorney with value of your home. A few short years ago, lenders were more than ready to make second mortgages or home equity loans. In this alternative, homes listed for sale would sell after one to three months, again making cash quickly available to the settling parties and their attorneys. Loans are now much harder to come by, eliminating a way to pay your attorney during the case, and homes stay on the market one year, two years, or indefinitely, tying up the parties' equity.

Under these conditions, it is harder for an attorney to represent you in a continuing case once the retainer is gone. Under almost all contracts between attorneys and clients, the attorney is allowed to expect an additional retainer once the first retainer is exhausted. In the alternative, some attorneys will not request an additional retainer, but will expect to be paid regularly throughout the case. Because overall access to funds and wealth is so reduced, very few attorneys will want to work very long if all they are getting is an increasingly large debt owed by the client. In some cases, the attorney's contract will require the client without a retainer to pay the balance due each billing period—either immediately, or within a certain number of days. Another popular contract provision provides that, once the debt owed to the attorney reaches a certain amount, the attorney will be allowed to withdraw from the case.

Thus, there is tension between the proper size of retainer and the client's ability to pay. If the retainer is too small (what I call a "doorbuster," after the practice of luring buyers in with an unreasonably low price), even a careful attorney who bills conservatively will easily exhaust the retainer, and either need a new retainer, or will wish to withdraw from the case. A larger retainer will keep the attorney in the case longer, and provide continuity and confidence for the client. Larger retainers can be harder to come by, or requiring a larger retainer may delay the filing of the case while a client saves or searches for funds. Even though unearned retainers are refundable, handing over the larger check often represents a greater extension of trust by the client, as well. Sometimes, a balance can be struck by the retainer being paid in phases. This can allow the attorney to get started sooner, while the client is contractually obligated to keep the funds coming.

Unless specifically stated by the attorney, a retainer usually is not reflective of the anticipated total costs of the case. More often, the retainer is designed to take the case from inception to a certain point in time or in the development of the case. In this instance, the strategy of the case and the wishes of the client are important. I like to make sure the retainer is sufficient to get a good feel for the case. If I can do so, I will be in a better position to evaluate further strategy and what further retainer will be needed to continue. If the goal is to draft the initial divorce paperwork (called the complaint or petition, or file a response if the client is the respondent), get the other party served, and get the initial exchange of financial disclosures done, then a certain level of retainer is warranted. If we take this approach, at the end of this "block" of the work, we will have a much better idea of the case ahead. At the completion of these steps, we will know if the other side is going to hire an attorney or not, we may not know the quality and experience of the other attorney, we will know how the other side has reacted to the filing, and we should know quite a bit about the finances. During this "file and conduct reconnaissance" phase, the case may develop in a variety of ways. A calm, amicable, and cooperative environment may develop— which is usually the client's hope and goal. In such an atmosphere, we can hope for a lower level of stress and an easier (and thus less expensive) case. On the other extreme, this phase can result in police involvement, orders of protection, moves to separate residences, custodial wrangling, and multiple motions. These developments, of course, result in a more intense and work-intensive case that will drive up fees. Because very few cases are predictable, especially in the early stages, this approach to the case and retainer can be very beneficial. Once this initial phase has been completed, the attorney should have a better understanding of what is at stake, how the opposition will litigate the case, and what sort of additional retainer is needed.

Some cases, by their nature, will require more than this approach from the very beginning. In cases where the home environment is unsafe or unhealthy to the parties and the children, legal proceedings to get the spouses in separate houses may be necessary. There may also be incidents that lead to police involvement, orders of protection, or other proceedings. Temporary (also known as "interim") relief motions may also be called for. Temporary custody motions can greatly add to the complexity and expense of a case. In some instances where custody is at issue, the parties can at least cooperate to such an extent that temporary custody can be handled by agreement while the overall custody determination is being litigated. If the situation is volatile, or the parties cannot agree on temporary residential arrangements, custody, parental rights, or visitation, then a myriad of rather expensive motions and litigation are needed. In the early stages of a case, temporary financial motions may also be needed. If the parties cannot agree on temporary child support, spousal support, payment of the bills, or the like, discovery of the facts and litigation of the disputes will be needed. In cases where there will be any level of temporary relief sought, the costs of the case, and the retainer required to pay these costs, will naturally increase—sometimes greatly.

Generally, any custody case will require a larger retainer. This is not simply because of the higher intensity and stakes involved in a custody battle. Additional steps and tools are brought into play in custody cases. These cases always have financial impacts that can come with them, so the custody case will certainly require extra work, and fees will be generated accordingly. In addition to the attorneys' fees involved in the custody case, other service providers will also likely be involved, such as *guardian ad litems*, children's representatives, attorneys for the children, testifying doctors or experts, and custody evaluators. For all of these reasons, retainers in custody cases are almost invariably higher.

An arrangement that is gaining acceptance and popularity is the flat or fixed fee. Under such a retainer arrangement, the attorney and client agree at the beginning of the case to a set price for the work to be performed. In a "bundling" arrangement, the attorney will agree to do a certain amount of work for a fixed price. The client can control costs, and the attorney can manage risk, as the client pays for only discreet tasks to be performed, rather than the uncertainty of continuing litigation. In what is usually called a flat fee case, the attorney agrees to represent the client for the entirety of the case for one set price, so long as certain conditions are met. In the most typical scenario, an attorney will agree to do all of the legal work required for the divorce for a set price, so long as the matter remains "uncontested." Usually, this sort of contract is entered into when the parties have agreed to most or all of the terms of the divorce, where there are either no children or no custody disputes because the children are grown, and where it is expected that no issues will be litigated at a trial or a contested hearing.

In most fixed fee contracts, the attorney earns and has the right to keep the entire retainer, regardless of how much time is spent on the case. Even in such a case, I think the attorney should keep track of the time spent, in the event there is some dispute or the case does not unfold as expected.

An area of concern in the contractual arrangement is what happens if the client changes his or her mind during the case, or wants to release the attorney during the case? In such an instance, a dispute can arise as to whether or how much of the flat fee the attorney can keep. Time records can be very helpful in resolving how much the attorney earned in representation under such circumstances. Illinois law and attorney ethical rules provide that attorneys in these cases can only keep the amount the attorney has reasonably earned.

Of course, not all cases that start out simple and undisputed end up that way. An agreement in advance needs to be reached as to what should be done if an "uncontested" case turns into a contested one. Many flat fee contracts provide that, if an uncontested case ends up being litigated, or if the parties do dispute issues, the flat fee contract is then converted into an hourly rate case.

3

Understanding the Issue of Grounds (Or "Why" a Divorce Is Sought)

Filing for divorce in Illinois is, after all, filing a lawsuit. Even if both parties agree to a divorce, one of the parties must still file a divorce petition and allege "grounds" or a reason that the divorce should be granted.

As I usually tell my clients, there are three ways to get a divorce in Illinois: the easy way, the hard way, and the very hard way. The easiest and by far most popular method of obtaining a divorce is through proving the grounds of irreconcilable differences. This is often times called a "no fault" divorce, as the petitioner is not required to allege or prove fault on the part of the respondent. In a no fault or irreconcilable differences divorce, the parties agree that the marriage is irretrievably broken down and cannot be saved. To accomplish such a divorce, the petitioner must allege:

1. That irreconcilable differences have caused the irretrievable breakdown of the marriage;
2. That past attempts at reconciliation have been unsuccessful;
3. That future attempts at reconciliation are not likely to succeed and are not in the best interests of the family; and
4. That the parties have lived separate and apart, and not as husband and wife, for a period in excess of six months from the date of the finalization of the divorce. (This does not require the parties to live in separate residences, as explained below.)

If the respondent agrees that the marriage is broken and cannot be saved, he or she agrees to sign a written agreement (called a Stipulation for

Waiver) that sets forth these points (see Stipulation for Waiver, Appendix G).

Many parties have a conceptual problem with the idea of the six-month separation. I often explain this requirement by telling the client that this requirement is more a matter of addressing the parties' "state of mind." After all, neither the court nor anyone else will come to check up on the parties to see if this requirement has actually been met. For the purposes of a divorce under irreconcilable differences, the parties can live in the same house (even be sleeping in the same bed), and still be "separated" for the purposes of grounds. As long as they both sign the stipulation, it is considered to be true and sufficient for the purposes of the divorce. If the client has any qualms about the intellectual honesty of signing the stipulation, I tell them to consider the stipulation as a statement that, for the last six months or so, their relationship has not been as it should be between a husband and wife. If this does not reassure the client, I remind them that it is quite possible that, from the date the divorce is filed to the date it is finalized, six months may well run, and they can consider that the six-month period of separation.

If both parties agree to the divorce under these grounds and will sign the stipulation, then sufficient grounds for the divorce exist, and no other grounds need to be alleged or proved. For this reason, if the divorce is to be agreed, it is not unusual for the divorce petition to be pled based only on the grounds of irreconcilable differences.

It is also common for a divorce petition to only allege irreconcilable differences if the petitioner is trying to set as amicable and non-judgmental an atmosphere as possible. If there is some uncertainty as to whether the divorce will be contested as to grounds, the petitioner may allege only irreconcilable differences in the hopes that the "no fault" allegations will prevent anger and acrimony.

The downside to the grounds of irreconcilable differences is that, to serve as grounds for the divorce, both parties must agree to the grounds and sign the stipulation. Even if the respondent agrees to the grounds themselves, he or she may refuse to sign the stipulation, because they disagree with some other aspect of the case. If the respondent is seeking leverage on issues like custody, maintenance, or the division of property, he or she may refuse to sign the stipulation. For this reason, the petitioner often alleges other grounds for the divorce.

If the respondent is unwilling to sign the stipulation, the petitioner can allege a two-year separation. This is the two-year "waiting requirement" that the parties waive in the irreconcilable differences divorce. To prove grounds of a two-year separation, the petitioner must allege and be able to prove at trial:

a. He or she is living "separate and apart" from his or her spouse;
b. Without fault; and
c. The petitioning party is in need of reasonable financial support from the spouse while they live apart.

To prove the two-year separation, the petitioner must be able to show, at a trial and by way of evidence, that the parties have lived separate lives to the degree required by the law. Typically, parties under these grounds will be living in separate homes. In fact, this set of grounds is most often used against an absent spouse. If your spouse has been missing for several years, the stipulation for irreconcilable differences, of course, cannot be signed by them, but one could prove that the parties have been separated for a period in excess of two years. Typically, a petitioner needs to show that there has been a sufficient separation of the parties' lives and finances to proceed under these grounds. In rare instances, parties can live in the same house and still be considered "separated" for the purposes of this provision of the law. This scenario is similar to when children divide a room or the back seat of the family car with an imaginary line. Needless to say, this "War of the Roses" scenario where the parties share a home for two years while fighting a divorce is fairly infrequent. Unfortunately, with recent economic turns, however, it is more common that parties do live together in the marital home during the divorce process.

A seemingly contrary provision of Illinois law is the requirement that spouses who are married are required to support the other. If so, even though a party can prove separation sufficient to establish grounds by having separate finances, parties can have intermingled finances and still prove separation for these purposes.

In point of fact, although often pled, very few cases are ever resolved on these grounds. In the large majority of cases, parties ultimately agree to sign the six-month stipulation, even if the respondent is initially unwilling to sign it. Where the respondent has some hesitancy about whether the divorce should be proceed or not, it is not unusual that the divorce process, or in extreme situations, the two-year wait, is usually pretty persuasive. Once the respondent agrees to the grounds of irreconcilable differences, there is no longer any need for the grounds of a two-year separation, and this count can be dismissed.

The final method of proving grounds is, at a trial, proving fault as spelled out in the statute. To prove "fault," the petitioner must prove, by competent evidence, that:

...without cause or provocation by the petitioner: the respondent was at the time of such marriage, and continues to be naturally impotent; the respondent had a wife or husband living at the time of the marriage; the respondent had committed adultery subsequent to the marriage; the respondent has willfully deserted or absented himself or herself from the petitioner for the space of one year, including any period during which litigation may have pended between the spouses for dissolution of marriage or legal separation; the respondent has been guilty of habitual drunkenness for the space of 2 years; the respondent has been guilty of gross and confirmed habits caused by the excessive use of addictive drugs for the space of 2 years, or has attempted the life of the other by poison or other means showing malice, or has been guilty of extreme and repeated physical or mental cruelty, or has been convicted of a felony or other infamous crime; or the respondent has infected the other with a sexually transmitted disease. "Excessive use of addictive drugs", as used in this Section, refers to use of an addictive drug by a person when using the drug becomes a controlling or a dominant purpose of his life;

In my experience, very few contested cases end up with a trial on grounds. Very few litigants go through the time, embarrassment, stress, and expense of a trial on grounds. The most frequent use of a trial on grounds is where the respondent is absent or does not participate in the trial, and the petitioner is not willing to wait the two-year period discussed above.

In contested cases, even where the respondent does not initially agree to the divorce, the prospect of a trial on grounds often leads the respondent to agree to the six-month stipulation of irreconcilable differences. Again, this is usually to avoid the expense and discomfort of a trial where the petitioner airs the marriage's dirty laundry in court. Of the grounds spelled out above, when fault grounds are used, mental and emotional or physical cruelty is by far the most popular. Although many cases involve suspected adultery or infidelity, actually proving adultery is more difficult than one might expect. It is far easier to prove mental and emotional cruelty, especially in cases where adultery is proven or suspected, and so adultery is less often used.

In virtually every case, the petitioner feels that he or she has sufficient proof that the other spouse has been guilty of one (if not several) of the behaviors that constitute fault-based grounds.

Because the petitioner is often hurt by these behaviors, and they have the natural desire to be vindicated, the petitioner will often want to include fault-based grounds in the petition. In some states, proof of fault correlates to financial benefits. In such "fault based" states, the petitioner can be awarded financial compensation in the divorce if he or she proves the other party guilty of fault. In Illinois, marital misconduct (or fault) has no bearing on finances or the division of property and debt, so unless proving fault will be necessary to establish grounds, the existence of fault is much less important in most cases.

It is important to note that the petition can be modified after it is initially filed. In fact, a petition can be modified right up until the final hearing of the case (which is called a "prove-up"). If a petition includes two or more counts (or grounds, as spelled out above), and the case can be resolved on one only (such as the signing of a Stipulation for Waiver and the use of grounds of irreconcilable differences), then the other counts can be dismissed. If the non-confrontational appeal of pleading only irreconcilable differences in the initial pleading is taken, and the respondent refuses to sign the stipulation, then the petitioner can add either the two-year separation set of grounds, or allege fault-based grounds.

4

Custody

For being such an emotionally charged and important issue in the break-up of a marriage, the legal concepts involved in custody are greatly misunderstood by most people. I am shocked by how little many of the litigants I encounter know about custody, even after they have been in a custody case for several months. For this reason, I like to spend a considerable amount of time in my initial consultation discussing exactly what custody is in Illinois law. By doing so, I can educate prospective clients, make sure we are "speaking the same language" when we discuss custody issues, and help shape their thoughts and expectations.

The first concept that needs to be explained is what "legal custody" means. Legal custody equates to the power of a party or parties to make major life decisions about a child's religion, education, and health care. If one has sole legal custody, that party has exclusive power to make decisions about the "big three"—major religious decisions, educational decisions, and health care decisions for the minors. If the parties share joint legal custody, they each have an equal vote as to these three issues. If the parties share joint legal custody but cannot agree to an issue, then Illinois law usually requires a three-step process to resolve the dispute. First, the parties must attempt to resolve the issues between themselves. If that does not work, in most instances, the parties have to attempt mediation to try to resolve the issue. If mediation fails, then the parties are able to litigate the issue in court. In this final circumstance, the court will hear evidence from both parties as to what they consider to be in the "best interests" of the children, before deciding how to resolve the disputed issue. As with all litigated issues, the danger in letting the court decide a disputed issue where the parties have joint legal custody is that instead of deciding in favor of one party or the other, the court may craft a solution that appeals to neither party. In all cases, where parties attempt to settle an issue, they at least remain in some control as to the outcome of the issue. Unfortunately, when the decision-making power is handed over to the court, the parties may lose all control over the process, and may give life-changing decisions to the court.

Joint legal custody is usually created by agreement of the parties, rather than because of litigation. It is possible to litigate the issue of legal custody, wherein one party seeks sole legal custody and the other party seeks joint legal custody; or where both parties seek sole legal custody; and have the court award joint legal custody to the parties. This is a fairly infrequent occurrence, however, since the essence of joint legal custody is a finding by the court that the parties can cooperate consistently and effectively to make decisions in the best interests of the children. If the parties fight vigorously over the issue, it is difficult for the court to find that the parties are able to cooperate consistently and effectively. A court will sometimes see beyond the heat of the battle, and find that the parties really have no fundamental disagreements as to religion, education, or health care. In this case, the court could decide that joint legal custody is acceptable.

More often, however, a court will decide that either the disagreement that led to the litigation - or the process of the litigation itself - ends up making good, consistent communication and cooperation unlikely.

Unfortunately, in custody, it is never more true that "it takes two to tango." It can be terribly unfair that one party's refusal to cooperate makes joint legal custody improbable or impossible. It seems to me that joint legal custody should be the preferred result if the parties do not have serious disagreements as to religion, education, or health care decisions regarding the children. The role of these three factors is discussed more fully in Chapter 1.

The issue of joint versus sole legal custody can be used as leverage by some parties. After all, a sworn pleading seeking sole legal custody certainly makes it seem as though the petitioner is alleging that the respondent is an unfit parent. As seen above, the idea and sound of the concept of "joint legal custody" is more imposing and emotionally impactful than actual legal custody is in everyday life.

Even a party who has had little or no involvement in making a child's major life decisions in the areas of religion, education, and health care might feel insulted by the suggestion that they should "lose" legal custody of their child. Not to be underestimated is the effect of social standing, family pressure, and the effect of "losing face" when the idea of legal custody is at stake. While the legal custody decisions may not be a significant real life issue to the parties, the social and emotional factors can loom large. For all of these reasons, a party may hold out on the issue of joint legal custody, suggesting that they are unable to share legal custody with the spouse, to coerce concessions and in other areas (the "cash for hostages" play).

The other aspect of custody is residential custody. The parent with residential custody is the parent with whom the child resides on a day-to-day basis. The other party, the "non-residential" parent, is said to have parenting time or visitation with the minor.

In most parenting agreements or judgments, the residential custodian makes the day-to-day decisions regarding the child. The other parent, especially in cases of joint legal custody, will often have input in these lesser decisions, but many times disputes or differences are resolved in favor of the residential parent.

The home of the parent with residential custody is usually considered the legal address of the child(ren), and is usually the house that determines where the child is registered for school. Another major aspect of residential custody is that the parent with residential custody is almost always entitled to child support from the non-residential parent. Child support is discussed more fully below in Chapter 5.

The issue of child custody is, of course, an extremely complicated matter, perhaps the most complicated issue in all of family law. Because of the introductory nature of this book, and its focus on how to prepare yourself for potential divorce litigation, the topic of custody litigation will not be addressed in any depth here. The subject of how to prepare for the custody aspects of the divorce litigation has already been the subject of many books, and could easily be an entire separate volume here. Handling divorce litigation is so highly dependent upon the facts, that any general advice will be very non-specific by nature. I would also be greatly inclined to defer to the advice of your attorney, since he or she will have a much better knowledge of the "lay of the land," and have a better understanding as to the disposition of judges in your jurisdiction.

For our purposes here, I think the best thing you can do to prepare for custody litigation is to review the ten "best interests" factors that will be pivotal in the decision. In resolving custody litigation, the court is charged with protecting your children's best interests. These best interests are defined as incorporating ten factors that the court must consider in deciding what is in the best interests of your child(ren) with regard to custody. These same factors apply to the decisions of legal custody, residential custody, and almost every other custody-type decision relating to your child(ren), such as visitation or other issues of parental rights. For this reason, you should have a very thorough and deep understanding of the ten best interests' factors, and how they might apply in your case. The ten best interests' factors, as individual factors, are especially important. The reason this is so is because, in the vast majority of cases, only a very few of the ten best interests factors apply. Although the court is allowed to consider other factors in assessing your child's best interests, the court is mandated to consider these ten factors, and so they are given a special weight. If only one, two, or three of these factors apply in your case, they will become especially important in the determination made by the court. Although these factors are all supposed to be weighted equally, a factor that does not apply in your case will, of course, have nothing to do with the decision. Local practice from court-to-court seems to give some unintended extra weight to certain factors, and so reliance upon your attorney's experience and judgment is important.

The ten best interests factors that he court must consider, in deciding your child(ren)'s best interests with regard to custody are:

1. The wishes of the child's parent or parents as to his custody;
2. The wishes of the child as to his custodian;

3. The interaction and interrelationship of the child with his parent or parents, his siblings and any other person who may significantly affect the child's best interest;
4. The child's adjustment to his home, school and community;
5. The mental and physical health of all individuals involved;
6. The physical violence or threat of physical violence by the child's potential custodian, whether directed against the child or directed against another person;
7. The occurrence of ongoing or repeated abuse as defined in Section 103 of the Illinois Domestic Violence Act of 1986[2], whether directed against the child or directed against another person;
8. The willingness and ability of each parent to facilitate and encourage a close and continuing relationship between the other parent and the child;
9. Whether one of the parents is a sex offender; and
10. Whether either party is on an active military duty.

Although I have had cases that involve all of the ten best interests factors, the ones that I think are most frequently central to custody litigation are Factor 2 (the wishes of the child), Factor 3 (the interaction and interrelationship of the child with his parents and others), and Factor 4 (the child's adjustment to his home, school, and community). A factor that I think some attorneys and litigants do not pay enough attention to is Factor 8, the willingness and ability of the custodial parent to facilitate and encourage a close and continuing relationship between the child and the non-custodial parent. While this factor can sometimes be hard to prove, and is often largely based upon speculation as to how the future will unfold, I consider this a somewhat "secret ingredient" to successful custody litigation, and I feel this is a factor that can influence judges and is often overlooked or underestimated by less experienced practitioners.

It is important to note that a party who is awarded primary residential custody ordinarily has the right to move anywhere with the child inside the boundaries of the state of Illinois. The party with residential custody, however, cannot move outside of the state of Illinois, without agreement by the other party or approval of the court. This can seem especially

---

[2] 750 ILCS § 60/103 (West 2012).

ironic and burdensome to the party wishing to move, when the state line is only a few minutes away, but they would be allowed to remove the child to a location five or six hours away within the state without any problem. This area of the law, called "removal," brings unique challenges and an additional set of laws to abide by during your divorce case. If you wish to reside with your child outside the state of Illinois, either immediately after the divorce, or any time in the foreseeable future, make sure that you discuss this issue with your attorney early on. The law of removal is a complicated and evolving one, and is very specific to the facts at hand. The decision whether you want to remove your child from the state is therefore a very important reason, as it may greatly complicate the time, expense, and difficulty of your case.

The parties can, however, negotiate some limitations on where the residential parent can reside within the state of Illinois. Often times, to reach an agreement, the parties will agree to reside within some agreed upon area after the divorce. In such a case, the parties might agree to reside in the same school district, county, or some other geographical area, following the divorce. The law would rarely, if ever, impose such a restriction on the residential parent, but it is perfectly allowable for the parties to agree to such a restriction, to resolve a custody dispute. One key element to this strategy point is the interaction between the proposed residential parent's desire to move out of the area, and Factor 4 of the best interests factors (the child's adjustment to his home, school, and community). A party cannot very well argue that their having residential custody will support the child's adjustment to home, school and community, while also expressing their desire to move to the other end of the state.

Staying in the House

Especially in a custody case, there are clear advantages to a party remaining in the marital home. If a party leaves the home and the children remain there, that party has an obvious disadvantage in a custody dispute under most circumstances. Remaining in the home is certainly more convenient, can be less expensive than moving to alternative housing, and provides other benefits. If the atmosphere in the house is unpleasant or unsafe, however, a party may want to remain in the house, but have the other party removed.

Laypeople seem to greatly misunderstand the legalities of "kicking someone out of the house." Often times, a spouse will tell the other to get out, and that party moves out voluntarily, even though under no legal obligation to do so. In some cases, this might be wise to diffuse a bad situation or help keep the peace. In other cases, there may not be a financial or custody risk to moving out, and the party seeking to move on with his or her life, or to avoid unpleasantness, may wish to voluntarily move out of the house. I strongly urge you to discuss moving out with your attorney before doing so, unless you have to leave the house to protect your or your children's safety. Under Illinois law, there are only two ways to force a spouse out of the marital residence. An order of protection is governed by the Illinois Domestic Violence Act[3]. Typically, an order of protection is sought on an emergency basis. Although orders of protection apply in other situations than our discussion of divorce, I will only discuss the aspects of an order of protection that directly relate to the idea of getting your spouse out of the house, or their efforts to involuntarily remove you from the home. In an emergency order of protection, the petitioner appears in court without any notice to the other party. The party seeking the emergency order of protection fills out a series of forms and usually testifies before the judge as to abuse or neglect by the spouse (or someone else with whom they have a certain legal or family relationship). If the judge is persuaded that sufficient abuse or neglect has or is likely to occur, an emergency order of protection may be issued. This is considered an extraordinary remedy, in that the accused, at least at this stage, is not notified of the allegations, and does not have the opportunity to challenge the allegations or to tell their side of the story.

If an emergency order of protection is issued, it is in place for no more than twenty-one days. At the end of the twenty-one days, a hearing will be held to see if the order of protection is to be modified as to its terms, and to see as to whether the emergency order of protection is extended. The court has the option of extending the emergency order of protection into an interim (or temporary) order of protection. Such an order can

---

[3] 750 ILCS §§ 60/101-60/401 (West 2012).

remain in place for no more than six months, and can only be renewed under very limited circumstances. An emergency order of protection can also be extended into a plenary order of protection, which remains in place for two years, or until further order of the court. Sometimes a plenary order of protection is in place for less than two years, as its terms can be modified by the final terms of the divorce. An emergency order of protection can provide the protected party with many remedies, including requirements that the defendant have no contact with the protected party, stay away from the protected party, or have no visitation or contact with the parties' children. The emergency order of protection can also grant the protected party exclusive possession of either a portion of the home, or the entire home.

At a later date, the accused has the opportunity to challenge the allegations and perhaps have the emergency order of protection dismissed, vacated, or at least have the terms modified to a more favorable arrangement. Because an emergency order of protection is issued (if granted), and the accused is removed from the home as soon as possible, this is one method by which a spouse can be legally removed from the marital home. Care must be exercised, since the unscrupulous can use this method to get an upper hand (especially in an anticipated custody battle) by making up false allegations to get the other party temporarily out of the home.

The second method for involuntarily removing a party from their home is a motion for exclusive possession. To obtain an order for exclusive possession, the moving party must prove:

> 750 ILCS 5/701. Marital residence – Order granting possession to spouse
>
> Where there is on file a verified complaint or verified petition seeking temporary eviction from the marital residence, the court may, during the pendency of the proceeding, only in cases where the physical or mental well being of either spouse or their children is jeopardized by occupancy of the marital residence by

both spouses, and only upon due notice and full hearing, unless waived by the court on good cause shown, enter orders of injunction, mandatory or restraining, granting the exclusive possession of the marital residence to either spouse, by eviction from, or restoration of, the marital residence, until the final determination of the cause. No such other order shall in any manner affect any estate in homestead property of either party.

Because the moving party must give the other side advance written notice of the motion and the non-moving party has the right to appear and defend themselves, a motion for exclusive possession is much harder to obtain. As the economy has gotten tighter, I believe motions for exclusive possession have been granted on an even less frequent basis. I think judges think it is much harder to find and afford alternative housing now, and so the judges are often more likely to admonish the parties to behave and to refuse to separate the parties under a motion for exclusive possession.

5

Current Trends in
Child Custody and Support

The most interesting current issues in Illinois family law, especially for those of us who practice largely in the area of custody litigation, relate to evolving concepts like shared residential custody, and the Illinois courts' changing approach to removal of children's residences from the state of Illinois. As we experience more "two-shift" families, or families where both parents have been very actively involved in the hands-on caregiving and upbringing of the children, more cases stray away from the more traditional model, where one parent is awarded primary residential custody and the other has "visitation."

I prefer to avoid the use of the term "visitation," as I do not think it is respectful of the parent/child relationship. A "visit" is when your uncle comes in from out of town. I think the term "parenting time" should be the preferred term. Because there are more cases where both parents have been active "hands-on" caregivers, we see more cases where the parties want to share residential custody.

Although there are no firm statutory guidelines for visitation, a "traditional" model once emerged where the non-residential parent would ordinarily expect to have parenting time on alternating weekends, and perhaps on one or two weeknight evenings. First, as a result of the increasing role of many fathers in the care and hands-on rearing of children, and then later as a result of more families where both parties work full time (or more), or worked different times of the day, the need to share residential custody arose. The idea of sharing residential custody, or at least providing the non-residential parent with more parenting time, was often recognition of economic and employment realities. Attorneys in this area have also encountered more parents who are willing to recognize the role and importance of both parents in the rearing of the children, and who have a genuine desire to share the upbringing of their children with their ex-spouse.

Illinois courts, at least some of those in the "collar counties" surrounding Chicago, appear to be increasingly receptive to this approach. The major issues that immediately come to mind with regard to shared residential custody or expanding parenting time for the non-residential parent are issues such as parenting schedules, transportation, and the very frequent interaction required between parents sharing residential custody. An important consideration that sometimes does not occur initially to the parties has to do with restrictions on where the respective parties will reside, to facilitate shared residential custody. While the parent having "primary residential custody" of a minor may reside anywhere in the state of Illinois that he or she wishes, giving either party latitude to reside anywhere within the state would certainly make shared residential custody difficult, if not impossible, in many cases.

For this reason, some Joint Parenting Agreements and Marital Settlement Agreements now include provisions restricting the parties as to where they can reside following the dissolution of the marriage. Interesting issues and negotiation points are raised by how to go about restricting the parties: whether by school district, particular school boundary lines, cities, counties, mileage restrictions, or the like. The tension here is between Part Five of the Illinois Marriage and Dissolution of Marriage Act's "best interests" standard regarding the "child's adjustment to his home, school and community,"[4] and the residential parent's right to move freely within the state. A party cannot claim to be the better residential custodian based on their commitment to maintaining the child's adjustment to home, school, and community, while also desiring to move out of the child's school district, neighborhood, or scout troop.

Ordinarily, another issue that arises out of the shared residential custody issue is that of child support. Illinois takes a very inflexible approach to

---

[4] 750 ILCS § 5/602(a)(4) (West 2012).

child support, wherein the "guideline" support amounts are very rarely deviated from.

Absent extraordinary circumstances (typically very high or very low income by the parent paying support, or unusual or special needs of the minors), child support in Illinois is calculated according to a strict and seldom varying formula. In this formula, gross income from all sources earned by the payor has subtracted from it certain statutory deductions, such as federal and state income tax, Social Security tax, Medicare tax, union dues, uniform fees, and a very few, other limited deductions. From this number, the payor's "statutory net income" is determined, and a fixed percentage of that statutory net income is paid as child support, based on the number of children. The party paying support will pay 20 percent of their statutory net income in cases involving one child; 28 percent in cases involving two children; 32 percent in cases involving three children; 40 percent in cases involving four children; and 50 percent in cases involving five or more children. In addition to this "statutory child support," which is intended to be used to purchase food, clothing, and shelter for the minors, child support also includes payment of the children's health insurance premiums (typically by the person paying child support, although this is sometimes shared by the parties), as well as contributions (usually by both parties) to the children's uncovered medical expenses, reasonable and necessary educational expenses, and reasonable and necessary daycare for the parties to work or attend school. Unlike some other states, Illinois does not consider the income of the spouse receiving support, and will only consider the needs or budget of the party receiving support in unusual cases. There have been frequent movements to change Illinois child support calculations to a formula that takes more factors into account. I believe Illinois will choose to change how child support is calculated eventually.

In cases of shared residential custody, and especially in cases where the parties approximate a 50/50 split of the child's parenting time, the issue arises as to who should pay child support to whom. Unfortunately, some courts look with suspicion on the shared residential custody proposal, because there is fear that it is an economic compromise between a party not wishing to pay full child support, and a party not wishing to litigate the child support or custody issues.

A frequent method for resolving child support issues in such cases is to compare the child support that one parent would have to pay to the other (for instance from the father to the mother) with the same amount that the other party would pay in child support (*i.e.*, the amount the mother would have to pay to the father). In these instances, courts will often accept an arrangement where the higher income parent's guideline child support (say, 20 percent of the father's statutory net income, for one child), has deducted from it guideline child support from the mother to the father (20 percent of the lower income parent's support is deducted from the larger support amount, resulting in the difference between the two support amounts). For example, let us say child support from the father to the mother (if she had full-time residential custody) would be $200 per week; and support from the mother to the father (if he were to have residential custody) would be $100 per week. In this "offset" approach, the father would pay the mother $100 per week (the difference between the $200 and $100 per week).

While there are some judges and courts that seem quite comfortable with this "offset" approach, others will not deviate from guideline child support, even when both parties share time equally. In a similar vein, there are judges and courts that will deviate by some percentage from guideline support, but not by the strict offset manner set forth above. If you are considering sharing residential custody with your spouse, you should discuss how child support would be handled with your attorney.

When deciding whether one party may remove the children to reside in another state pursuant to a dissolution of marriage (and in family law/paternity cases, likewise), Illinois courts were formerly guided almost solely by the "direct benefits" standard. Recent case law and trends, however, have shown openness to considering "indirect" benefits to the children, when deciding whether removal is in the children's best interests. Courts will still initially review the proposed removal, to ensure that the proposed removal is not solely for the purpose of interfering with the other party's parenting time or parenting rights. Once this threshold has been crossed, the courts will then review the proposed direct and indirect benefits to the children, should such a removal be permitted.

Thus far, it has been difficult in many cases to predict how a court will decide the removal issue. Assuming that the removal is not proposed simply for the purpose of frustrating the other parent's parental rights, courts seem to be more readily able to grasp economic arguments in favor of or against removal. In such situations, the parent seeking removal might seek to present evidence showing that they have better chances of employment, higher earning potential, better chances for advancement, or other professional benefits resulting in the move to another state. In a similar vein, the parent seeking removal may seek to prove that the target state has a lower cost of living, or would otherwise result in a higher standard of living for the parent and the children. While some parties want to focus on the fact that the proposed new state is somehow superior, or a better place to raise children, than the jurisdiction where the case is being litigated, I am always hesitant to try to tell a judge that the county where I, and most likely the judge, are raising our children is deficient, and that our children would be better served by living somewhere else.

Determining the difference between the direct and indirect benefit approaches often leads to some hazy line drawing. Returning to an area where the family was originally from, or where the parent seeking removal has family, friends, and a support network, is frequently offered as a direct benefit to the children. It can also be viewed, in certain fact patterns, as more of an indirect benefit, by showing that the parent with residential custody will have better daycare, more financial and emotional support, or will otherwise benefit from being around family, with resulting benefits for the well-being of the children.

By being more willing to consider the indirect benefits of the move, I believe the courts are presenting a more liberal approach to removal, and allowing for more consideration of the interests of the parties, as well as the best interests of the children. This is not to say the indirect benefits approach ignores the children's best interests, or places the parents' desires over the best interests of the children. Rather, it may represent a more realistic view of the family dynamic, and the fact that a happy residential custodial parent who enjoys benefits such as family and a support network, better employment, a lower cost of living, or the like, may result in a better upbringing for the children.

It seems as though one sure fire way to increase the chances of a successful removal is for the party seeking removal to be married to, or be planning to be married to, someone firmly rooted in a favorable situation in another state.

The Illinois Marriage and Dissolution of Marriage Act and the Illinois Supreme Court Rules, as well as most Circuit Court Local Rules, now mandate that child custody issues be given priority and resolved promptly. The newly enacted provisions[5], which aspire to have custody issues resolved and Parenting Agreements entered into within eighteen months, provide that if such issues cannot be promptly resolved, cases are immediately sent to mediation, and then to a trial date. Custody issues are mandated to be resolved, via settlement, mediation, or trial within eighteen months of the filing of the petition, unless written findings are entered by the court as to the cause for delay. Some courts have been easing into this requirement, while other courts appear to favor a strict approach to this major shift. While I think all parties would agree that resolving child custody issues first is in the best interests of the children, and also makes economic sense (since issues such as who is going to reside in the marital residence, who is going to pay child support, and the like certainly affect the financial issues in the case), the time frame mandated seems to be too short in some cases. I believe practitioners are tailoring their approach to cases involving children to better meet the demands of these new laws, but I think the transition will be a gradual one. It is fair to expect your attorney to make custody and child support issues among the top priorities. But so far, it is often *not* reasonable to expect that complex custody disputes will always be resolved within eighteen months of filing.

Another factor at work is the inherent tension between the intense emotions and difficult issues involved in a custody matter, versus the incredibly prohibitive price of most custody litigations to the average client. I think that the "fast track" approach and the new laws may be forcing people to make the custody decisions in their cases more quickly. While that might save court time and legal fees, it may also lead to more "compromise" agreements that are not well thought out or in the best

---

[5] ILCS S. Ct. Rules 900-908, 921-23 (West 2012).

interests of the children. While it is certainly good to avoid the expense and trauma of child custody litigation where possible, I hope that recent changes and trends will not lead to ill-advised decisions or decisions where the parties reach "compromises" wherein they are "splitting the baby," rather than actually resolving the matter in the best interests of the minors.

Visitation, Parenting Time, and Parental Contact

As previously mentioned, I prefer not to use the term "visitation." I think it is disrespectful to the parent/child relationship to call a parent's time a "visit." While this may just be me, my clients seem to have latched onto the idea, as well. In my part of the state, we have certainly gotten away from the "traditional" every-other-weekend pattern for parenting time. Although these schedules are still used, I would estimate that they are a rather small minority. As there are more and more "two shift" families, or families where both parents have been very actively involved in the rearing and day-to-day care of the children, the parties' expectations for time spent with their children post-decree have changed.

I believe this is in the best interests of many children, and I think this will probably result in further changes to our custody laws down the line. Our current custody and parenting time laws are fairly unstructured, leaving much to the parties and the discretion of the court. I think that litigators and the court are now much more sensitive to the fact that a child needs both parents, and needs face-to-face and day-to-day involvement for the child's betterment. As we get away from the every-other-weekend model, unique issues arise. If a party is going to exercise weekday parenting time, the practical realities of work schedules, school schedules, extracurricular activities, meals, and sleep all come into play.

Early on, I will sometimes review with my client a twenty-eight-day, four-week calendar. We begin by blocking out the time that my client is (hopefully) at work, because that does not really represent parenting time. After that, we block out times that the child is in school or asleep. Although I certainly understand the joy of tucking in your children, peeking in while they are asleep, or seeing their cheerful faces first thing in the morning, a good argument can be made that overnights are not really quality parenting time. While more and more litigants seem to expect weeknight overnight parenting time, this is met with varying acceptance by our courts. This seems to be driven largely by the age of the child, and the expectations of the court.

In my experience, many courts frown on overnight parenting time during the school week. I think more judges are adopting the attitude that, during the school week, a child should have "one bed." This is especially true for grade school and middle school-aged children. I have seen judges show more latitude with preschoolers and high school-aged children, in terms of weeknight, overnight parenting time. Like many aspects of joint parenting, this of course depends on the proximity of the parents, and especially their willingness to work together. I have personally been involved in a case where a child, by the parents' agreed schedule, changes residences twenty-two times a month. I think many would consider this an extreme example. While this child appears to have turned out to be a well-adjusted, happy, and successful child, I am not sure this schedule would work for many children. I think the use of week on/week off or similar alternating schedules is also on the wane. Again, I think this is a function of the court's recognition that school-aged children require a certain amount of stability and consistency in their lives. There are, of course, cases where the parties can cooperate to such a high degree that a "50/50" split can work, but I would say that this is true in a minority of cases.

Courts are very willing to accept the idea of what we refer to as "evening" parenting time, such as from after school or 5:00 p.m. until about 8:00 p.m. or so. This allows the parent and child to enjoy "quality time," but also preserves some stability during the child's school week. During summertime and other school breaks, of course, a more liberal approach seems to work well. Some of our custody evaluators and child psychologists have told us that school-aged children should, at a minimum, see each parent at least once every two to three days. Afternoon or evening parenting time can be used creatively to make sure that this occurs. As mentioned above, a party driving hard for a 50/50 split of parenting time may be viewed with some suspicion, because that party might be angling for a reduction or elimination of child support, at the expense of stability and upbringing of the child. In better financial times, we have seen cases where parties have rented an apartment or bought a separate home, so that the parties can rotate which parent resides in the home and which parent resides in the "bachelor/bachelorette pad." I am also aware of a case where parties have each bought a new home, and preserved the marital home, allowing the children to remain there, while the parents rotate in and out. These cases, of course, are extreme, and increasingly rare in the current economy.

Newer ideas, such as "Internet visitation" (I am more willing to call this visitation, and not so much parenting time) have been introduced. In my experience, I have yet to see Internet visitation be accepted as anywhere near the equivalent of actual parenting time. Of course, our courts encourage the parties to provide for and foster day-to-day telephone contact (or Internet contact) with the children and the party not in possession of them. Unfortunately, I have seen more game playing with telephone visitation than with in-person parenting time. It seems that the ability to screen calls, ignore voice mails, or otherwise "dodge" the other parent is something that some parties are more than willing to engage in.

This leads to the need for creative solutions, such as purchasing cell phones specifically for the children's use in communicating with the other parent, or creating strict telephone visitation time schedules. Although there are some parties who are willing to manipulate this factor, I think most find it exhausting and give up before long. The use of the telephone, Skype, a web cam, or any other media for communication between the child and the absent parent is worthwhile, but is often overestimated. As media savvy and as "wired" as our children are, it is often tough to get them on the phone to talk to mom or dad.

6

Evaluations in Custody Disputes

Determining who will be involved in a custody dispute is a very important strategic decision. Often times, this will be governed or determined in part by your court's local rules, or at least local practice. There are three statutorily created entities that can become involved in a child custody dispute. The most frequently used entity in my area (Kane, Kendall, DuPage, Will, and DeKalb counties) is the *guardian ad litem* (GAL). Although the law also provides for a child representative and an attorney for the child, these are infrequently used in my region. If your case will involve a custody dispute, ask your attorney to explain what the practice in your area is.

The child's representative is an attorney, appointed by the court, who is charged with advocating for the child's best interests. The child's representative, however, is the one who determines what is in the best interests of the child, and then acts as an attorney and advocate, pursuing the result that he or she feels is in the child's best interests. The attorney for the child, however, is also appointed by the court, but serves a different function. The attorney for the child also advocates for the best interests of the child, but does so at the direction of the child. This represents a somewhat unique situation, in that the experienced family law litigator is now taking marching orders from a minor, based on what the minor feels is in his or her best interests. In areas where these two statutorily created creatures are disfavored, it is my impression that judges feel that these sorts of advocates place too much power either in the hands of the child's representative, or in the hands of the child herself. Another factor that I am sure comes into play is the fact that mom and dad in a custody litigation are most likely already financially strapped from paying their own counsel, and perhaps a *guardian ad litem* and custody evaluator. Adding yet another attorney, in the form of a child's representative or attorney for the child, would greatly add to the expense of an already costly proposition.

In my region, a major decision facing litigators is whether to use a GAL, a custody evaluator, or both. A GAL is (usually) an attorney who is experienced in family law, has received special training, and has been selected by the judge to serve, often with input from the attorneys. I believe that many cases are well served by the appointment of a *guardian ad litem*. A *guardian ad litem* usually provides a more common sense view of the issues, is more likely to provide the court with specific and concrete facts on which to base a decision, is usually faster, and is almost always less expensive and intrusive than a custody evaluator. Of course, the quality of a *guardian ad litem*'s investigation varies from case to case, and certainly from guardian to guardian.

It seems that most judges have a good grasp of which guardians will serve best in a particular case, as well as preferences for certain *guardian ad litems'* styles or output. Some judges will expect an oral or written report from the GAL, and judges will also advise the guardian whether or not recommendations as to custody are requested by the court. I find my work as a *guardian ad litem* especially rewarding. It is intellectually and professionally interesting to be deeply involved in a case where one does not have a personal stake in the outcome. Acting as a *guardian ad litem* provides a litigator with insights into the case, litigants, counsel, and custody litigation generally that one does not ordinarily benefit from when involved in a case as a litigator.

By law, the *guardian ad litem* has fairly broad powers and abilities, and can also be called to testify at trial. An effective *guardian ad litem* can be a great asset in resolving custody disputes, big and small. In fact, in many cases, the mere appointment of a *guardian ad litem* (which involves the parties, often both of them, paying a significant retainer to the GAL) is enough to settle custody issues. I have experienced many instances, both as a litigator and as a *guardian ad litem,* where apparently litigation-bound parties quickly resolve custody issues when the *guardian ad litem* is appointed, the process is explained, and the retainer is requested. In cases where guardians are actually activated, if their investigation is thorough and their report well founded, the parties will often be guided by the opinion of the *guardian ad litem*, and can thus resolve cases more quickly. Where a guardian does a clearly insufficient report, where weaknesses can be readily pointed out in their methodology, or when the guardian is unable to make a clear determination, the guardian's report is easily subject to attack by either or both parties.

Some courts automatically refer custody cases to a custody evaluator, although this is a dying trend in my area. Custody evaluators are selected by the court, and are most often psychologists or psychiatrists with specialized training in this area. Tied closely to the experience level of the custody evaluator is the fee involved. It is not uncommon for a custody evaluation to run from $3,000 to $5,000, sometimes more. By then, the economic realities can be daunting to many litigants, and the appointment of a custody evaluator often changes a client's appetite for litigation in this field. Although custody evaluators vary in their approach, it has been my experience that they are much more likely to rely on the objective and subjective psychological tests they administer, and seem to be less "fact driven." While evaluators will interview the parties and other witnesses, this seems to be less a factor in the evaluator's decision.

This can certainly lead to a different result than the report of a *guardian ad litem*. It is not uncommon for a *guardian ad litem* and a custody evaluator to come down on opposite sides of a decision. In many cases, a custody evaluation proves to be more intrusive for the parties and the children than a GAL's investigation would. For these reasons, many courts feel it is the best practice to try to resolve custody decisions through the investigation by a *guardian ad litem* first. In the event that the GAL is unable to reach a clear conclusion, or in the event that the court or parties cannot be persuaded by a guardian's report, then a custody evaluator is likely to be appointed.

Care should be exercised by the attorneys when deciding to employ a custody evaluator, and deciding which custody evaluator to employ. I think there are many attorneys who believe they have a good "feel" for certain custody evaluators, and that their cases can benefit by the selection of a particular evaluator. One of the dangers involved in choosing to use a custody evaluator is the perception among many attorneys that a custody evaluator's opinion is given an undue amount of weight by the court. There may be something to the fact that a custody evaluator presents a "more scientific" opinion than a *guardian ad litem* in creating this perception. The *guardian ad litem* cannot point to elevated scales of certain personality traits on an MMPI (Minnesota Multiphasic Personality Inventory), a test score, or any other objective data. Of course, many courts are aware that even the best custody evaluations employ an imprecise science, and are only one of many guides that a court should consider. Based upon the expense involved in a custody evaluation, the intrusive nature of a custody evaluation, and the potential bias that may result from an unfavorable report, litigators should take great care in deciding whether a custody evaluation is appropriate in their case, or at a particular stage in their case.

7

Discovery

Discovery is the process of exchanging financial and other information. There are a variety of levels of discovery, each more thorough, but also more time-consuming (and expensive) for you and your attorney to pursue. Many courts in Chicago's "collar counties" rely on a Comprehensive Financial Statement, or some similar document, which provides somewhat detailed, but not "scorched earth," financial disclosures. The counties in this area will require you to fill out an eight- to fifteen-page document intended to set forth a "snapshot" of your income, tax deductions, monthly budget, debts, and assets. In cases where counsel can complete these accurately, provide the appropriate support documentation (W-2, wage stubs, retirement account balances), and exchange them quickly, cases are much more likely to settle or avoid expensive discovery.

Some counties do not permit other formal written discovery (such as Interrogatories and Requests for Production, which are discussed below) until these financial statements are exchanged. This rule is not always strictly enforced, but I think in many cases it represents the best practice for efficiency's sake. When parties promptly exchange accurate and appropriately documented Comprehensive Financial Statements or the like, I think the prospects for settling division of property and debt, child support, maintenance, and other important financial issues can occur quickly. In cases where the parties are unable to resolve these issues after exchanging this level of discovery, more pinpointed, "laser" discovery can be requested. I believe that attorneys can turn cases around more efficiently, and at a lower expense, when full-blown discovery can be avoided. Obviously, there are cases where Interrogatories, Requests to

Produce, depositions, Request to Admit, and other forms of discovery are appropriate. The exchange of complete and documented Comprehensive Financial Statements, where they do not lead to prompt settlement, can certainly make things like pretrial settlement conferences more productive by narrowing issues, leading to factual stipulations or sparing the expense of discovery.

Marital Interrogatories are a series of written questions served on the opposing party. These written questions are required to be answered, also in writing, within a limited time period. Although answers to interrogatories are technically due within thirty days, it is not at all unusual for this time period to be continued. A party's written answers to interrogatories are signed by the party, under oath. For this reason, interrogatories must be answered carefully and reviewed thoroughly by the party, before they sign them and send them along to opposing counsel.

Marital Interrogatories usually address basic issues in the case, such as questions about employment, education, assets, debts, and other financial matters. The Illinois Supreme Court has created form interrogatories that are to be used for this purpose, unless the court grants specific permission for different interrogatories to be used.

There are two main purposes to obtaining an opposing party's written answers to interrogatories. The primary purpose is to obtain information from the other side. This is the "discovery" part of discovery. By answering interrogatories, the opposing party gives a formal, written, and sworn to answer to the questions that are asked. This will allow both the party and the attorney to have a greater knowledge about the case, and about the other party's understandings of things like assets, debts, and other financial issues.

The second purpose to written interrogatories is to "ice" the opposing party's testimony. When a party gives a particular written and sworn answer to an interrogatory, it will be very difficult for that party to give a contrary answer in the future. Although, of course, facts and financial information do change over time, the use of written interrogatories is a good way to "beat down" your opponent's answer. If the opponent gives a written answer, under oath, in their interrogatories, this can be used to contradict (or "impeach") the party if they try to testify differently during a deposition, or at a hearing or trial.

Another popular form of discovery is a Request for Production of Documents. A Request for Production of Documents can be one of the most aggravating and cumbersome parts of the divorce process for many parties. Requests for Production of Documents are not standardized, like the Illinois Supreme Court approved interrogatories are. Requests for Production of Documents, like most forms of discovery, can be very far ranging, and do not always address issues that seem to be relevant to your case. Essentially, a Request for Production of Documents is an often lengthy laundry list of all of the documents or tangible arguments that opposing counsel wants you to produce to him or her. A typical Request for Production of Documents could include something like a request for you to produce the last three years' worth of all of your cancelled checks, your paystubs, copies of bills, or statements from different accounts. When served with a Request for Production of Documents, the responding party is essentially responsible for two kinds of documents: those documents in the party's possession, and those documents under a party's control. That is to say, if you do not keep copies of your last three years' worth of bank statements, you cannot refuse to produce them by saying they are not "in your possession." Most often, documents like this would be "in your control," in that you could contact your bank or other financial institution, and have them make you copies of such documents. Although a court can prohibit certain requests if they are found to be harassing or unduly burdensome, this form of discovery is usually given very broad latitude, and you can be asked to produce voluminous amounts of virtually every kind of record you can imagine. It should be noted that that Requests to Produce can also include other sorts of tangible items, such as photographs, video tapes, or other types of tangible evidence. Although it typically takes longer to respond to a Request for Production of Documents, ordinarily these responses are initially required within thirty days of you receiving the Request for Production of Documents.

The last form of discovery with which you should be familiar is a deposition. Depositions usually occur after the preceding forms of discovery have been completed. In a deposition, the party being deposed appears before the attorney seeking the deposition, accompanied by their attorney, if they have one. It is also typical for the opposing party (i.e., your spouse) to also be present at the deposition. During the deposition, the opposing attorney has up to three hours to ask you virtually any question you can imagine. Again, you are somewhat protected from abusive or harassing questions, but the scope of discovery is very broad, and you would be prepared to expect the unexpected in terms of questions to be asked. While your attorney is there to protect you from abuse and harassment, and may object to certain questions, giving a deposition is still usually considered a very intense and stressful experience.

While your deposition is being given, a court reporter is present, taking down every word said by you, your attorney, and opposing counsel. The taking of a deposition is a very expensive process, as it will involve fees for both attorneys, their preparation for the deposition, and the fee for the court reporter to attend the deposition. The court reporter will then later charge an additional fee, if the deposition transcript is to be written up, or if you would like copies of the deposition transcript. In many cases, attorneys and their clients seek to avoid depositions, because they are lengthy and expensive affairs. While there are other forms of discovery that you may encounter in this process, these are by far the most common, and ones with which you should be aware.

8

Factors Affecting the Decisions Whether and When to File

There are many ways that a client can benefit by filing a Petition for Dissolution of Marriage in the state of Illinois. These include the ability to better control the litigation, the opportunity to have first crack at defining the terms and pace of the case, and the chance to prevent dissipation of assets. The concept of "dissipation" of the marital estate is an evolving one. Until recently, "dissipation" of the estate was measured from a date that the court determined the marriage to have been "broken down." The process of determining exactly when a marriage "broke down" was certainly an art, rather than a science. Most litigators would agree that a bright line for identifying the date of dissipation, at least under the former approach, would be to look to the date of the filing of the petition. In such a case, a client would be advised that any property or money spent, wasted, or destroyed by the opponent prior to the date the marriage broke down would be held to have occurred during the marriage, and not compensable. If, however, the other spouse spent money for a non-legitimate, non-marital purpose, or incurred debt or destroyed assets for a non-legitimate, non-marital purpose, and did so after the date of the petition for dissolution (or other "break down" date, as determined by the court), then the spouse could expect the court to compensate the wronged spouse for this damage to the marital estate. Under the past practice, filing a petition for dissolution of marriage was a solid way to establish a date for the marriage to have broken down, and thus to judge the financial misdeeds of a spouse going forward.

Recent developments have led to a change in the approach of the courts. The courts have recently found dissipation can begin from the time that a marriage *begins* to breakdown. While this certainly creates more possibilities, it also makes it much more difficult to establish a date when dissipation begins. I personally have experienced a case in which my client firmly believes the marriage began to break down over the course of the honeymoon. An interesting issue of fact can be presented to the court with regard to when a marriage *began* to break down. Complicating this will be attempts at reconciliation, smooth periods where the parties are not in conflict, or multiple, repetitive instances where breakdowns in the marriage occur. To argue dissipation in either approach, however, a divorce petition does need to be filed. The court will not involve itself in your family or finances if a divorce or legal separation is not on file.

Illinois parenting and custody law becomes much more clear, once a divorce petition has been filed. There are many instances where a party unilaterally makes decisions regarding a child, removes a child from the marital residence, or otherwise engages in "aggressive parenting." Without a divorce petition or petition for legal separation on file, neither the police nor the courts can do much to protect the parties' "co-ownership" of the child. Until the provisions of the Illinois Marriage and Dissolution of Marriage Act or court orders are in place, there are few real rules governing the conduct of a parent with regard to a child. Lack of rules, certainty, and a method of enforcement can create a very chaotic situation, which is especially stressful to the child. Once a petition for dissolution of marriage is filed, however, not only does the law impose certain requirements and restrictions, but also interim orders can be sought to govern parenting during the divorce. The "fast track" approach to custody discussed above will certainly assist the practitioner whose client is willing to get the case on file, in a case where the child is being used as a pawn, or one parent insists on acting unilaterally, to the disregard of the other party or the child. An advantage to being the party who files the petition for dissolution of marriage first is that it allows the party to set the tone of the case, and stake out the battlefield.

For a party seeking joint legal custody and a peaceful resolution, custody and other issues can be framed in their pleadings in an appropriate fashion, to reassure the other party. A pleading seeking joint legal custody, or even shared residential custody, is less likely to fan the flames, than a pleading asking for "sole care, custody, education and control" of the child. There are still many practitioners who frame their initial pleading in the manner most favorable to their client, asking for things like sole legal custody, maintenance, payment of attorneys' fees, or other elements that the client does not even truly desire or expect. In my opinion, this is not necessarily being "lawyerly," but somewhat intellectually dishonest. Pleadings can always be modified to conform to the facts of the case, so I do not see any need to ask for the moon in filing initial pleadings. I think the odds of successful compromise and negotiations are more likely when the initial pleadings are framed in a manner consistent with the client's true objectives. Your attorney's approach may be different, but I do not think starting at the extreme ends and "dickering" is productive, efficient, or respectful.

Additionally, by being the first to file, in Illinois, the petitioner is in a position to voluntarily dismiss the case, with the option to re-file later in most instances. I have encountered cases in other states where both parties must agree to voluntarily dismiss a case. Of course, when one is the respondent, that same choice is lacking. I advise clients who are convinced their marriage is over that it is advantageous to be the one who files, simply because the petitioner is in a better position to control the speed of the case. The ability to voluntarily dismiss a case, or even the specter of that ability, is a legal, as well as psychological, advantage with some clients.

A frequent alternative that clients ask about is filing for a legal separation. Legal separation is infrequently used in Illinois, although it has utility in certain situations. A legal separation is frequently used in cases where the parties are not religiously permitted to divorce, and more frequently, when health insurance or pre-existing medical conditions are an issue. Parties who need to remain married for insurance purposes, especially while a party is treating for a serious medical condition, will sometimes seek a legal separation to resolve marital conflict, while helping to preserve health insurance benefits or medical treatment. When parties are not fully resolved to the dissolution of the marriage, legal separation can of course be a benefit. A petition for legal separation would allow the court to enter orders regarding finances and child custody/upbringing, which can provide structure and order during times of marital discord. The parties are then, perhaps, better able to work out issues or reconcile.

9

Mediation, the "Uncontested" Divorce, and Settlement

Mediation is now required in child custody cases, where the parties cannot promptly reach a joint parenting agreement resolving all parenting issues. As such, it is a much more frequent part of our practice then even a year or two ago. The value of mediators or mediation seems to be driven primarily by two factors: the abilities of the individual mediator, and the mindset of the parties entering into mediation.

Most litigators agree that there are times and issues that are perfectly suited for mediation. Also, many attorneys will tell you that there are situations or parties where mediation is an utter waste of time and money. While mediation is required in custody cases that cannot be quickly resolved, it is often short-lived where the parties are firmly entrenched. In Illinois, mediation can only be conducted by trained and appointed mediators. I am more and more often called by clients looking for an inexpensive and non-confrontational resolution to their divorce, who ask if I am willing to meet with both of them and "mediate" their divorce. I find that most often the parties misunderstand the idea of mediation, and are not, in fact, really seeking it.

In a typical situation, one party will call me, and let me know that the parties have reached agreement on all issues, and want their case resolved as quickly and amicably as possible. They often request that "mediation" be used to resolve their case. This is, of course, not what mediation means. In these cases, I advise the client that mediation is for when you *do not* agree, and you need a third party neutral to see if a compromise can be reached. Although there are some who believe that mediation should be the first step, I do not think this is necessarily efficient or in the best interests of the parties.

If parties were to meet with a mediator and work everything out, it is still likely that counsel would be necessary to prepare the appropriate documents and conduct a prove-up of the divorce. It is possible that the parties can represent themselves, but very few people are comfortable doing so, and many find that they are unable to meet all of the court's requirements for self-representation through completion of the divorce. Since an attorney will have to be involved at some point, if the parties truly are amicably resolving the case, I do not see any reason that an attorney cannot be utilized from the beginning. In such cases, a simple, one-count petition for dissolution of marriage (alleging irreconcilable differences) can be prepared. The non-represented party should sign a waiver of service that acknowledges the attorney does not represent this party, and has not given this party any advice. The waiver will acknowledge that the party has the right to be served by the sheriff or private process server, but instead wishes to be served by counsel, his office, or by mail. The party retaining the attorney can then explain the terms of the proposed dissolution of marriage to counsel.

This is a critical point in terms of trust and success in these "agreed" divorces. As the client/lay person explains, in whatever detail possible, the terms of the proposed settlement, it is not uncommon that the parties have forgotten or were unaware of important elements. Both the parties have come to this point, believing that they are in full agreement and that everything can be resolved based on the contents of the wrinkled spiral notebook paper that they brought into the attorneys' office. When the attorney alerts the party he represents as to missed issues, such as handling tax consequences of various aspects of the divorce, or dividing retirement benefits in a proper fashion, the parties are often surprised to find that there is some issue that they have not considered. If the correct atmosphere exists between the parties, and the attorney can present the issue in a proper fashion, this is often not fatal to a smooth and amicable resolution to the case.

Unfortunately, some non-represented parties (or even some represented parties) view this as an intrusion by the attorney, and an attempt to "churn the file" by creating conflict where there was none. When something like this happens, a mediator can be very useful. By resolving as many issues as possible, counsel can then turn the parties over to the mediator, to resolve any new issues or issues to which agreement cannot be reached. A mediator can assure both parties that the issue raised by counsel is a legitimate one that should definitely be addressed in their settlement. In an instance such as this, a mediator can be an efficient, inexpensive solution that will lead to greater trust by the parties. Any agreement that comes out of trust and negotiations by the parties, of course, is more likely to be abided by and lead to the satisfaction of all parties involved.

There are, of course, some issues that are clearly not susceptible to mediation. Ultimate custody determinations, in my experience, can seldom be resolved through mediation. Parenting time schedules and other aspects of parenting time, where one is not asked to "split the baby" seem to be better suited to mediation. Although it is certainly possible to address financial issues successfully in mediation, this seems to occur less frequently. For some reason, it has been my experience that parties do not seem comfortable or successful in using mediation to resolve their financial issues. I think this will evolve as time goes on, and mediation becomes a more familiar part of the process.

The reason mediation is less successful in financial matters is based upon the fact that most financial decisions are driven by objective facts, and thorough documentation. Mediation, at least as it is currently practiced, seems to better address the emotional and parenting issues involved in a case, and is less about chugging the numbers, reviewing discovery, and reaching some agreement as to important financial decisions. The pretrial settlement conference is frequently used as an extra-litigational way to resolve disputes.

After sufficient discovery and negotiation have been conducted, counsel typically prepares a pretrial memorandum to submit to the judge. This document, which can be anything from a single page to a volume of multiple exhibits, sets out the facts that the judge needs to know about the case and the litigants, and then spells out each party's position and proposed resolution. Some courts do not require pretrial memorandums; some attorneys do not provide them, even when they are required. I can see very few situations where a written pretrial memorandum is not warranted. For the judge to give the attorneys good input as to the potential resolution of a case, a firm grasp of the facts is essential. If this is important enough to take up the time of both litigators and the judge in chambers, should not the judge have a concise written set of the facts in front of her?

If the parties can succeed in agreeing to the essential facts, or if the judge arrives at a grasp of the facts based on the opposing presentations in pretrial, most of our judges will discuss the issue with counsel before giving a recommendation. On occasion, the court will direct counsel to speak with their parties during the course of the pretrial (which is why I always expect my clients to be available, in-person where possible, during pre-trials). On other occasions, I have had the court ask to speak to one or both of the parties. Unless it is impossible or extremely difficult, I think it is always advisable for you to be available for the pretrial settlement conference.

There are, of course, situations where the judge is unable to give the attorneys a recommendation. I have found in most cases, however, that the judge is able to give a clear recommendation regarding the disputed issues. Clients seem to have a good common sense understanding of the recommendation process. Parties need to understand that the judge's "opinion," while not binding, is also not likely to change. After a pretrial settlement conference, I tell the client which facts were shared with the judge, the basis on which the judge made his or her decision, and what the judge's recommendations were. I explain to the client that the judge will keep an open mind and hear evidence if this matter comes to trial, but I feel the judge has a good grasp of the facts and law. In such a situation, it is usually wise for you to follow the judge's recommendation, as her opinion is not likely to change when she is presented with the same facts many months and tens of thousands of dollars later. A pretrial settlement conference can be the most effective way to resolve your case, if it is well conducted and the facts are presented in an organized fashion.

The Client's Role in Settlement

The most difficult thing for some clients to do is get past the notion of percentages or what it takes to "win" in a dispute. Especially with regard to financial matters, I take a budget-driven approach, because it is what the client has to spend and live on each month that matters, not what the percentage of a pie chart was awarded in a document in the clerk's dusty file. I do encourage clients to try to resolve issues amongst themselves to the extent possible. When there is bullying or abuse, this is of course not possible. This is also not possible where there is no level of trust, or parties are being dishonest about the numbers or facts. Where the parties can communicate honestly with each other, however, any issue they can resolve themselves is an issue well resolved. As I have said before, parties are more willing to live by agreements that they have helped forge, and feel more personally invested in them. An "agreement" to which a client does not agree feels like it is being imposed on her, rather than as part of a compromise.

10

Frequently Asked Questions

Q: **How does one initiate a divorce in Illinois?**

A: The person who wants to obtain a divorce is called the "petitioner," or sometimes the "plaintiff" or "complainant." Petitioner is the most frequently used term. This person files a written document that contains allegations of fact, such as the parties' names, the dates of the marriage, and information about the children and assets and debts. The petition finishes with what is called a "request for relief," which sets out what the petitioner is seeking, such as to have the marriage dissolved, to have custody of the children resolved, etc. The petition is filed with the clerk of the circuit court, and a summons is issued. The summons and petition are served on the other spouse, who is typically called the "respondent," or another term used is "defendant." The respondent is usually served with the summons and complaint by the county sheriff or a private process server. In some instances, arrangements are made so that the respondent does not have to be served in this fashion, but they instead accept the paperwork either directly, through the mail, or through their attorney. Once the respondent has been served with the summons and petition, they are required to file a "response" or "answer." The response contains their answers to the allegations of fact, and also contains a request for relief, where the respondent asks the court to either deny the divorce petition, or to grant it, but under different terms.

Q: **Do I have to be represented by an attorney?**

A: Illinois Law provides that, in virtually all cases, parties are free to represent themselves. This applies in all areas of family law. If a party chooses to represent themselves, it is said that they represent themselves on a *"pro se"* basis. This is a Latin term, which means "on one's own behalf." A *pro se* litigant is treated exactly the same as an attorney by the courts. A *pro se* litigant is expected to know the law, as well as all courtroom procedures and all of the technicalities of both divorce law and practice. For this reason, it is often extremely difficult for a *pro se* litigant to represent themselves, especially in court. In some cases, both parties choose to represent themselves. Although this offers no competitive advantage to either side, it is often difficult for the judge or court system to work with a case where neither party is represented by an attorney, especially if neither party is familiar with divorce or the court's procedures. The disadvantage of not being represented is compounded, when the other side is represented by competent counsel.

Q: Can we both be represented by the same attorney?

A: I am frequently asked this question, and more clients are asking this question in today's difficult economic times. It is illegal and unethical for an attorney to represent opposing sides in the same transaction. Any attorney who offers to do so would be subject to discipline, and should certainly be avoided. It is not uncommon for one party to be represented, while the other party represents themselves on a *pro se* basis (see above). In an uncontested case where the parties are essentially in agreement as to all issues, the arrangement where one side is represented by an attorney and the other side is *pro se* can be both fair and workable. In this case, the attorney represents only the party who has retained him. In such an instance, the attorney can communicate with the spouse who is representing herself *pro se*, as though she were another attorney. Accordingly, the attorney can prepare documents on behalf of his or her client, and can explain them to the opposing party. The attorney cannot, however, give advice or legal counsel to the opposing party.

Q: What should I do if I receive a petition for divorce in Illinois that my spouse has filed?

A: It is not advisable to try to avoid service of process. If you are aware that a sheriff or private process server is trying to serve you with a divorce petition, it is best to be cooperative and accept the pleading without trying to "duck" service. Once being served, the spouse who receives the complaint should probably consult with an attorney who focuses their practice in family law. After you are served with a petition for dissolution of marriage, you have thirty days to file an appearance (a legal document that identifies yourself or some other person as your attorney), and an answer to the petition (see above). If an answer is not filed within thirty days, you can be held in default, and the divorce can be granted to the other side, without your having any input in the result. If enough time passes after a default judgment is entered against you, it essentially becomes irreversible. This is why, even in a case where you feel that the parties may reconcile or you do not want to proceed with the divorce, it is essential to consult with an attorney promptly, before the thirty-day deadline runs.

Q: What are the alternatives to divorce?

A: A party can seek a legal separation, although this is not frequently done. The advantages and disadvantages of a legal separation are discussed more fully above. If a legal separation is obtained, the parties remain married, but the party seeking the legal separation has the right to live in a separate location. Parties who are legally separated can still be obligated to financially support each other, can still be responsible for the other's debts, and are still considered married parties in all other ways. Illinois Law also provides for the declaration of invalidity of marriage. This is the concept that many people call "annulment." Under certain, very limited terms, a marriage can be declared invalid. In the case the marriage is declared invalid, it is as though the marriage never occurred.

Q: Must a husband and wife live in separate residences when the divorce complaint is filed?

A: No. In fact, it is not unusual for the parties to live in the same residence until the time of divorce, or even until some time thereafter. In the current real estate market, there are instances where parties have been divorced for a considerable time, but continue to live in the same residences.

If the parties agree to the divorce on a "no fault / irreconcilable differences" basis, there is no need for the parties to ever live in a separate residence during the divorce proceedings. If, however, a party is unwilling to sign the stipulation agreeing to a "no fault / irreconcilable differences" divorce and the party seeking the divorce does not want to proceed with a trial on grounds, then the party seeking the divorce must be able to prove that the parties have lived separate and apart for a period in excess of two years. In certain, rare instances, parties can reside in the same residence for two years, but still be considered "separated" for the purposes of this two-year requirement. In such an instance, the parties typically totally separate their personal and financial lives, while continuing to still reside in the same physical residence for the purposes of either the children or financial benefit.

Q: Will I have to appear in court as part of my divorce?

A: At a minimum, you will need to appear in court for the final hearing, which is called a "prove-up." In cases where a divorce is settled by agreement, the attorneys prepare a parenting agreement (where there are children), a marital settlement agreement, a judgment, and usually, a stipulation for waiver. A stipulation for waiver is used when the parties agree to the grounds of irreconcilable differences, and wish to waive a trial on grounds and waive the two-year waiting period. When all issues have been resolved and the documents signed, Illinois courts then conduct the prove-up. At the prove-up, the parties appear before the court, testify that they understand the settlement terms and feel that they are fair, and briefly review the settlement before the judge. If the judge finds the settlement legally adequate and fair, then the divorce judgment is entered and the marriage is dissolved. The person seeking the divorce, or petitioner, is required to appear at this hearing, and the respondent, or other spouse, almost always appears as well. It is possible, however, for the respondent to waive, or give up his or her right to appear at the final hearing. If there are contested issues during the divorce, or if the divorce cannot be resolved by a settlement and has to go to trial, then the parties are required to appear in court. In some jurisdictions, judges also require the parties to be in court for pretrial settlement conferences or in other instances.

Q: If the parties cannot settle the case between themselves, who decides the contested issues?

A: In Illinois, juries are never used in family law cases. All cases are resolved by a judge. In most divorces, the parties will ultimately settle all issues between themselves, have their attorneys prepare the appropriate settlement documents, and the judge will review the documents to make sure that they are legally adequate and are essentially fair and not unconscionable. In such an instance, the judge reviews the documents to ensure that the children's best interests and support are being protected, and also reviews the documents to make sure that they are fundamentally fair. In such an instance, the judge will typically approve the documents without too much input. In cases where the parties are unable, however, to resolve issues, the judge hears the testimony of witnesses, reviews any physical exhibits, and then makes a decision that is binding on the parties.

Q: How long does it take to get a divorce?

A: If the parties reach full agreement and waive all waiting periods or other technicalities, there is no formal "waiting period" under Illinois Law. A divorce completed in three to six months would ordinarily be considered a very quick divorce. Many more divorces fall in the nine to twelve-month range. Some more complicated divorces can last two to three years, or even longer, but these are not typical. To a large extent, how long the divorce takes depends on how honest and up front the parties are about disclosing information, and how quickly they are willing to resolve the matter.

Q: Can I move to another state, with or without my child?

A: Setting aside the issue of children, an adult party is free to leave the state following a divorce. Assuming that an adult party, especially the Petitioner, has met the residency requirements to file their divorce, it is possible for a party to leave the state during the divorce. At least one of the parties must meet the relevant residency requirement at the beginning of the case, for the Illinois court to have jurisdiction over the case.

Neither party is allowed to remove the children, on a permanent basis, without the permission of the court or written agreement of the parties. The parties will sometimes need to temporarily remove the children from the state, for vacation or other purposes. This can be done by agreement of the parties or their attorneys, either on a formal or informal basis. To permanently remove the residence of the children from the state, however, the parties either have to reach an agreement, or the court has to grant permission. The idea of permanently removing the children from the state is called "removal," and is a complicated and evolving area of the law. Basically, whether or not the children will be allowed to be removed from the state is judged not by the interests of the parties, but by the best interests of the children. The court will also consider the interruption of the relationship and parenting time between the parent who will remain the in the state and the children.

Q: How is child support calculated and what is my obligation?

A: In Illinois, statutory child support is based on a formula and a set of guideline amounts. The guideline amount of child support is rarely deviated from, and can only be deviated from with the permission of the court. The parties alone cannot decide to deviate from guideline child support, as the court is charged with protecting the children's welfare, and the court has final say so on all child support arrangements. Therefore, even if the parties agree to an amount of child support, the court still has final say.

Child support is based on the statutory net income of the non-custodial parent. The statutory net income is computed by taking the payor's gross income from all sources, and then deducting properly calculated federal taxes, state taxes, Social Security taxes, Medicare taxes, union dues, health insurance premiums for the children and certain other, very limited deductions. After taking these allowable deductions from the gross income, the payor's statutory net income per pay period is established. Then a certain percentage of that statutory net income is set as child support, based upon how many children are involved. Guideline child support is 20 percent for one child, 28 percent for two children, 32 percent for three children, 40 percent for four children, and 50 percent of statutory net income for five or more children. The children are entitled to child support until they turn eighteen, or graduate from high school, whichever comes later. If an eighteen-year-old is still in high school, statutory child support continues until that child graduates or turns nineteen. Statutory child support is paid to the custodial parent, and is to be used for the food, clothing, and shelter of the children. The parent receiving child support is not obligated to account for the child support, and does not need to prove to the other parent how the child support is being spent. In addition to statutory child support, the non-custodial parent can be required to contribute toward the children's health insurance premiums, uncovered healthcare costs, and reasonable educational and daycare expenses. These additional types of child support are not included in the statutory percentage, but are considered separate obligations of child support. The income of the party receiving child support is almost never taken into consideration. The calculation of child support under current Illinois Law is very inflexible, and is very closely overseen by the courts.

Q: Am I obligated to pay for my child's post-high school education?

A: It has been said that Illinois Law offers a "gift" to the children of a divorce. Whereas the children in an intact family have no legal right to petition the court for money for college, children in a divorced family have this power. Either parent, or the child, can file a petition under Section 513, asking the court to decide who will pay for college expenses. Typically, once the court is convinced that the college expenses are reasonable and appropriate, the court will then divide the college expenses between each parent and the child. The child's contribution to his or her college expenses is typically covered by things like grants, scholarships, tuition waivers, loans, or employment. The court will look at the respective incomes and financial conditions of the parents, and then will usually order contribution by each parent to the child's expenses. There is no hard or fast formula for deciding these percentages, and the court takes many factors into consideration.

APPENDICES

APPENDIX A

CHECKLIST OF RESOURCES

	During pending divorce	
	Short term/after divorce	
	Long term/after divorce	

CHECKLIST OF RESOURCES

		DO I NEED		DO I HAVE		WHO / WHERE
		Yes	No	Yes	No	
SHELTER						
Place for me (self)						
Safe, short term place if I need to get out						
Place for children						
Safe, short term place for children						
HEALTH						
Insurance	Self					
	Children					
Medication coverage	Self					
	Children					
Short term meds supply	Self					
	Children					

Insurance policy information	Self						
	Children						
List of covered providers	Self						
	Children						
Insurance cards	Self						
	Children						
List of doctors	Self						
	Children						
List of medications	Self						
	Children						
List of medical conditions / history	Self						
	Children						
List of allergies	Self						
	Children						
INCOME / FINANCIAL SUPPORT							
Personal income							
Child support							
Temporary maintenance / alimony / spousal support							
Long term maintenance / alimony							
Loans							

OTHER SOURCES OF LIQUID FUNDS						
Checking account						
Savings account						
Money market funds						
Other bank accounts						
Cash on hand						
401(k) or other retirement savings						
Other						
Valuables (for sale)						
PERSONAL / EMOTIONAL SUPPORT						
Family support						
Friends support						
Church / religion support						
Counseling / mental health providers						
Work / Employment / Assistance						
Attorney (divorce)						

Attorney (other), family business, will/estate						
Accountant / Attorney / Bankruptcy						
Tax preparation						
Banker						
Financial Planner						
CFP						
Credit Counselor						
WORK / EDUCATION						
Employment opportunity						
Advancement at job						
Additional training or education through job						
College degree or _____ degree						
Community College / associates degree						
Temp or placement agency						
CHILD RELATED						
Counselor at school						

Counselor - other							
Babysitter / daycare (for work schedule)							
Class for self re coping with children and divorce							
Class for kids							
OTHER RESOURCES							
Things I have that will assist me at this point in my life:							
1)							
2)							
3)							
4)							
5)							
6)							
Things I need, but do not have:							
1)							
2)							
3)							
4)							
5)							
6)							

Creating a list like this may be intimidating at first, as you come to realize all that is needed and what you may lack. But, it may also be reassuring, when you realize the reserve already at your disposal. It may also be calming if the list itself becomes a resource, and you utilize it to go about completing the tasks you will need. Like most things in the divorce process, this list can grow and change as your situation evolves.

APPENDIX B

AFFIDAVIT OF INCOME AND EXPENSES

IN THE CIRCUIT COURT OF THE SIXTEENTH JUDICIAL CIRCUIT
KANE COUNTY, ILLINOIS

Case No._____

Plaintiff/Petitioner	Defendant/Respondent	File Stamp

AFFIDAVIT OF INCOME AND EXPENSES

A. Name: _____ B. Date of Marriage: _____

C. Children of the Parties (names & ages): _____

D. Are parties separated? ☐ Yes ☐ No If yes, date of separation _____ E. Custodial Parent: _____

F. Monthly Income (if paid weekly, multiply by 52 and divide by 12 to get monthly figures):

Place of Employment: _____ Monthly Gross: _____

Federal Income Tax: _____ State Income Tax: _____ F.I.C.A.: _____ MED F.I.C.A.: _____

Other involuntary deductions: _____ Specify: _____

Voluntary deductions: _____ Specify: _____

Number of exemptions claimed: _____ Monthly income from other sources (specify): _____

_____ Monthly Net Income: $0.00

G. Cash on hand (savings, checking, etc.): _____

H. Basic Household Monthly Expenses:

1. Rent or Mortgage	8. Car: Plates/Sticker/Repair _____	14. Food _____
2. House/Renters Ins. _____	9. Gas (car) _____	15. Medical/Dental _____
3. Real Estate Taxes _____	10. Car Payment _____	16. Clothing _____
4. Gas (house) _____	11. Car Insurance _____	17. Other Ins. (specify below) _____
5. Electric _____	12. Child Care _____	_____
6. Water/Garbage _____	13. Education (specify below) _____	18. Recreation and Travel _____
7. Telephone _____	_____	19. Cosmetic, Drugs, Beauty Care _____

20. Other monthly creditor payments (specify creditor, balance & monthly payments):

(Enter the total of these monthly creditors payments on line 20)   20. _____

Miscellaneous (specify):   21. _____

(Enter the total on line 21)   Expense Total _____

Difference _____ $0.00

STATE OF ILLINOIS COUNTY OF KANE

Under penalties as provided by law pursuant to Section 1-109 of the Code of Civil Procedure, the undersigned certifies that the statements set forth in this instrument are true and correct, except as to matters therein stated to be on information and belief and as to such matters the undersigned certifies as aforesaid that he/she verily believes the same to be true.

Date: 6/25/12   _____

Signature of Party

P5-D-011 (06/10)   [Print Form]

APPENDIX C

COMPREHENSIVE FINANCIAL STATEMENT (CFS)

IN THE CIRCUIT COURT OF THE SIXTEENTH JUDICIAL CIRCUIT
KANE COUNTY, ILLINOIS

Case No. _____

Plaintiff(s)	Defendant(s)	File Stamp

COMPREHENSIVE FINANCIAL STATEMENT
PURSUANT TO LOCAL RULE #15.13 (c)
INSTRUCTIONS

(1) All questions require a written response. If you do not have the information requested or do not know the answer to a particular question, indicate that as your answer.

(2) Use additional sheets if necessary.

(3) Attach copies of all supporting documentation in your possession.

Petitioner/Respondent, _____, being duly sworn, states that the following is an accurate statement as of _____6/25/12_____, of his/her net worth (assets of both parties), a statement of income from all sources, a statement of monthly living expenses, a statement of health insurance coverage, and a statement of assets transferred of whatsoever kind and nature and wherever situated:

Name: _____   Telephone No.: _____

Address: _____   Social Security No. (last 4 digits only): _____

_____   Date of Birth: _____

Date of Marriage: _____   Date of Dissolution of Marriage:

Date of Separation: _____   (if applicable) _____

Children of this marriage:

_____ age _____ residing with _____

_____ age _____ residing with _____

_____ age _____ residing with _____

_____ age _____ residing with _____

Current Employer: _____   Address: _____

Self Employment: _____   Address: _____

Other Employment: _____   Address: _____

☐ Check if unemployed

Number of Paychecks per year (Please Select One) ☐ 12 ☐ 24 ☐ 26 ☐ 52 ☐ Other _____

Number of Exemptions Claimed: _____

Number of Dependents: _____

Gross income from all sources last year: _____

Gross income from all sources this year: _____

STATEMENT OF INCOME as of _____

GROSS MONTHLY INCOME

Salary/wages/base pay	_____ Line 1
Overtime/commission	_____ Line 2
Bonus	_____ Line 3
Draw	_____ Line 4
Pension and retirement benefits	_____ Line 5
Annuity	_____ Line 6
Interest income	_____ Line 7
Dividend income	_____ Line 8
Trust income	_____ Line 9
Social Security Payments	_____ Line 10
Unemployment benefits	_____ Line 11
Disability payments	_____ Line 12
Worker's Compensation	_____ Line 13
Public Aid/Food Stamps	_____ Line 14
Investment income	_____ Line 15
Rental income	_____ Line 16
Business income	_____ Line 17
Partnership income	_____ Line 18
Royalty income	_____ Line 19
Fellowships/stipends	_____ Line 20
Other income (specify) _____	_____ Line 21

SUBTOTAL GROSS MONTHLY INCOME
(Total of lines 1-21) _____ Line 22

Additional Cash Flow (monthly)

Maintenance received _____ Line 23
(payments received prior to judgment or support orders in other actions)

Child support received _____ Line 24
(payments received pursuant to Court order or voluntarily in this or other actions)

SUBTOTAL ADDITIONAL CASH FLOW _____ Line 25
(Total of line 23 and 24)

TOTAL MONTHLY GROSS INCOME FROM ALL SOURCES _____ Line 26
(Total of line 22 and 25)

*

REQUIRED MONTHLY DEDUCTIONS

Federal Tax (based on _____ exemptions)   _____ Line 27

State Tax (based on _____ exemptions)   _____ Line 28
FICA (or Social Security equivalent)   _____ Line 29

Medicare Tax   _____ Line 30

Mandatory retirement contributions required by law or as
conditions of employment   _____ Line 31

Union Dues (Name of Union _____)   _____ Line 32

Health/Hospitalization Premiums   _____ Line 33

Prior obligation(s) of support actually paid pursuant to Court Order   _____ Line 34

TOTAL REQUIRED DEDUCTIONS FROM MONTHLY INCOME   _____ Line 35
(Add lines 27 through 34)

NET MONTHLY INCOME   _____ $0.00 Line 36
(Line 26 minus line 35)

STATEMENT OF MONTHLY LIVING EXPENSES as of _____

1. Household

   a. Mortgage or rent (specify) _____   _____ Line 37
   b. Home equity loan/Second mortgage   _____ Line 38
   c. Real estate taxes, assessments   _____ Line 39
   d. Homeowners or renters insurance   _____ Line 40
   e. Heat/fuel   _____ Line 41
   f. Electricity   _____ Line 42
   g. Telephone (include long distance and cell)   _____ Line 43
   h. Water and Sewer   _____ Line 44
   i. Refuse removal   _____ Line 45
   j. Laundry/dry cleaning   _____ Line 46
   k. Maid/cleaning service   _____ Line 47
   l. Furniture and appliance repair/replacement   _____ Line 48
   m. Lawn and garden/snow removal   _____ Line 49
   n. Food (groceries, household supplies, etc.)   _____ Line 50
   o. Liquor, beer, wine, etc.   _____ Line 51
   p. Cable/Satellite/Internet   _____ Line 52
   q. Other (specify) _____   _____ Line 53

SUBTOTAL HOUSEHOLD EXPENSES   _____ Line 54
(Total of lines 37 through 53)

MONTHLY LIVING EXPENSES CONTINUED

2. Transportation
   a. Gasoline — Line 55
   b. Repairs — Line 56
   c. Insurance/license/city stickers — Line 57
   d. Payments/replacement — Line 58
   e. Alternative transportation — Line 59
   f. Other (specify)_____ — Line 60

   SUBTOTAL TRANSPORTATION EXPENSES — Line 61
   (Total of line 55 through 60

3. Personal
   a. Clothing — Line 62
   b. Grooming — Line 63
   c. Medical (after insurance)
      1. Doctor — Line 64
      2. Dentist — Line 65
      3. Optical — Line 66
      4. Medication — Line 67
   d. Insurance
      1. Life Insurance Premiums — Line 68
      2. Medical/Hospitalization Insurance Premiums — Line 69
      3. Dental/Optical Insurance Premiums — Line 70
   e. Other (specify)_____ — Line 71

   SUBTOTAL PERSONAL EXPENSES — Line 72
   (Total of line 62 through 71

4. Miscellaneous
   a. Clubs/social obligations/entertainment — Line 73
   b. Newspaper, magazines, books — Line 74
   c. Gifts — Line 75
   d. Donations, church or religious affiliation — Line 76
   e. Vacations — Line 77
   f. Other (specify)_____ — Line 78

   SUBTOTAL MISCELLANEOUS EXPENSES — Line 79
   (Total of line 73 through 78)

MONTHLY LIVING EXPENSES CONTINUED

5.   Dependent children: Names and Ages

Name   Age

_____ ____

_____ ____

_____ ____

_____ ____

Children's separate expenses

a. Clothing   _____ Line 80

b. Grooming   _____ Line 81

c. Education

    1. Tuition   _____ Line 82

    2. Books/fees   _____ Line 83

    3. Lunches   _____ Line 84

    4. Transportation   _____ Line 85

    5. Activities   _____ Line 86

d. Medical (after insurance):

    1. Doctor   _____ Line 87

    2. Dentist   _____ Line 88

    3. Optical   _____ Line 89

    4. Medication   _____ Line 90

e. Allowance   _____ Line 91

f. Child care/after school care   _____ Line 92

g. Sitters   _____ Line 93

h. Lessons and supplies   _____ Line 94

i. Clubs/summer camps   _____ Line 95

j. Vacation   _____ Line 96

k. Entertainment   _____ Line 97

l. Other (specify) _____   _____ Line 98

SUBTOTAL CHILDREN'S EXPENSES: _____ Line 99

(Total of line 80 through 98)

TOTAL MONTHLY LIVING EXPENSES: _____ Line 100

(Add lines 54, 61, 72, 79 and 99)

STATEMENT OF CURRENT DEBTS/LIABILITIES (not previously listed on pages 1-5)

Creditor's Name	Purpose of Debt	Balance Due	Monthly Payment	
Add a line	Monthly Debt Service	$.00	$.00	Line 101

RECAP		
NET MONTHLY INCOME (Line 36)	$.00	Line 102
TOTAL MONTHLY LIVING EXPENSES (Line 100)		Line 103
DIFFERENCE BETWEEN NET INCOME AND EXPENSES (Line 102 minus 103)	$.00	Line 104
LESS MONTHLY DEBT SERVICE (Line 101)	$.00	Line 105
INCOME AVAILABLE PER MONTH (Line 104 minus 105)	$.00	Line 106

STATEMENT OF HEALTH INSURANCE COVERAGE

Currently effective Health Insurance Coverage: ☐ Yes ☐ No

Name of Insurance Carrier: _____ Policy or Group No. _____

Type of Insurance: ☐ Medical ☐ Dental ☐ Optical

Deductible: Per Individual _____ Per Family _____

Persons covered: ☐ Self ☐ Spouse ☐ Dependents

Type of policy: ☐ HMO ☐ PPO ☐ Standard Indemnity (i.e. 80/20)

Provided by: ☐ Employer ☐ Private Policy ☐ Other Group

Monthly Cost: Paid by Employer _____ Paid by Employee _____

For dependents _____

For myself _____

POTENTIAL DEBTS/LIABILITIES

Creditor's Name	Purpose of Debt	Anticipated Debt	Anticipated Monthly Payment	
				Add line

Cash or Cash Equivalents:

1. Savings or Interest Bearing Accounts

Name of Bank and Account Number	Title in name of	Date Acquired	Value/Amount	
				Add line

2. Checking Accounts

Name of Bank and Account Number	Title in name of	Date acquired	Value/Amount	
				Add line

3. Certificate of Deposit

Name of Bank and Account Number	Title in name of	Date acquired	Value/Amount	
				Add line

4. Money Market Accounts

Name of Bank and Account Number	Title in name of	Date acquired	Value/Amount	
				Add line

5. Cash

Name of Bank and Account Number	Title in name of	Date acquired	Value/Amount	
				Add line

6. Other (specify)

Name of Bank and Account Number	Title in name of	Date acquired	Value/Amount	
				Add line

INVESTMENT ACCOUNTS AND SECURITIES:

1. Stocks

Description	Title in name of	Date acquired	Value/Amount	
				Add line

2. Bonds

Description	Title in name of	Date acquired	Value/Amount	
				Add line

3. Tax Exempt Securities

Description	Title in name of	Date acquired	Value/Amount	
				Add line

4. Secured or Unsecured Notes

Description	Title in name of	Date acquired	Value/Amount	
				Add line

5. Mutual Funds or Brokerage Accounts

Description	Title in name of	Date acquired	Value/Amount	
				Add line

6. Other (specify)

Description	Title in name of	Date acquired	Value/Amount	
				Add line

SAFE DEPOSIT BOX:

Name of Bank, City, Box Number	Keyholder	Contents	Date acquired	Value/Amount	
					Add line

REAL PROPERTY:

1. Residence

Address of Property	Title Holder	Date acquired	Mortgage Lien Holder(s)	Mortgage Amt. Remaining	Fair Market Value	
						Add line

2. Secondary or vacation residence

Address of Property	Title Holder	Date acquired	Mortgage Lien Holder(s)	Mortgage Amt. Remaining	Fair Market Value	
						Add line

3. Investment or Business Real Estate

Address of Property	Title Holder	Date acquired	Mortgage Lien Holder(s)	Mortgage Amt. Remaining	Fair Market Value	
						Add line

4. Vacant Land

Address of Property	Title Holder	Date acquired	Mortgage Lien Holder(s)	Mortgage Amt. Remaining	Fair Market Value	
						Add line

5. Other (specify)

Address of Property	Title Holder	Date acquired	Mortgage Lien Holder	Mortgage Amt. Remaining	Fair Market Value	
						Add line

MOTOR VEHICLE(S), BOAT(S), TRAILER(S), ETC.

Year, Make, Model	Title in name of	Date acquired	Lien Holder(s)	Value	Loan Balance	
						Add line

BUSINESS INTERESTS: Type of entity, i.e. Corporations, Partnerships, Sole Proprietorships

Business Name/Type of Business	In name of	Date acquired	% Interest/ # of Shares	Value/Amount	
					Add line

INSURANCE POLICIES: Type of insurance, i.e. Life, Medical, Disability, Business Overhead, Property, etc

Name of Company/Policy Number	Name of insured	Date acquired	Beneficiary	Value/Amount	
					Add line

RETIREMENT, PENSION PLANS, IRA ACCOUNTS, DEFERRED COMPENSATION, ANNUITIES, 401(k), PROFIT SHARING, etc.:

Name of Company/Type of Plan	Participant	Vested Y/N	Date acquired	Beneficiary	Value/Amount	
						Add line

STOCK OPTIONS, ESOPs, OTHER DEFERRED COMPENSATION OR EMPLOYMENT BENEFITS: (Describe fully)

Description	Title in name of	Date acquired	Fair Market Value	
				Add line

INCOME TAX REFUNDS: Federal and State (current or expected)

Federal/State/Taxpayer Name	Joint or Individual	Tax Year(s)	Refund Amount	
				Add line

PENDING CLAIMS FOR PERSONAL INJURY, WORKER'S COMPENSATION, BANKRUPTCY, OR OTHER LAWSUITS, CLAIMS AND/OR DEMANDS SEEKING MONETARY AWARD(S) OR OTHER RELIEF:

Claimant	Nature and Amount of Claim	Date of Occurrence	Name and Address of Attorney	
				Add line

COLLECTIBLES: Coins, stamps, art, antiques, etc.

Description	Title in name of	Date acquired	Value/Amount	
				Add line

ALL OTHER MARITAL PROPERTY: Personal or Real, NOT PREVIOUSLY LISTED, valued in excess of $500.00 excluding normal household furniture and furnishings)

Description	Title in name of	Date acquired	Fair Market Value	
				Add line

NONMARITAL PROPERTY: Identify all property claimed to be nonmarital

Description	Title	Date acquired	Inheritance(I) or Gift(G) Premarital (P)	Value/Amount	
					Add line

STATEMENT OF ASSET TRANSFERRED: (List all assets transferred in any manner during the preceding six (6) months)

Description of Property	To Whom Transferred and Relationship To Transferee	Date of Transfer and Purpose	Value/Amount	
				Add line

CERTIFICATE OF DOCUMENT PRODUCTION

I, _____, certify that the attached document(s) are all of the documents I have in my possession or that I can obtain upon reasonable effort as of this date. The undersigned certifies that he/she has read the above and foregoing Comprehensive Financial Statement; that he/she knows the contents thereof, and that the information therein contained is true and correct.

☐ I have provided copies of all supporting documents in my possession, relating to the disclosures made above.

_____
Signature of Party ☐ Petitioner ☐ Respondent

_____
Type or Print Name

[Print Form]   [Clear Form]

APPENDIX D

STATEMENT OF CLIENT'S RIGHTS
AND RESPONSIBILITIES

(1)   **WRITTEN ENGAGEMENT AGREEMENT.** The written engagement agreement, prepared by the counsel, shall clearly address the objectives of representation and detail the fee arrangement, including all material terms. If fees are to be based on criteria apart from, or in addition to, hourly rates, such criteria (e.g., unique time demands and/or utilization of unique expertise) shall be delineated. The client shall receive a copy of the written engagement agreement and any additional clarification requested and is advised not to sign any such agreement which the client finds to be unsatisfactory or does not understand.

(2)   **REPRESENTATION.** Representation will commence upon the signing of the written engagement agreement. The counsel will provide competent representation, which requires legal knowledge, skill, thoroughness and preparation to handle those matters set forth in the written engagement agreement. Once employed, the counsel will act with reasonable diligence and promptness, as well as use his best efforts on behalf of the client, but he cannot guarantee results. The counsel will abide by the client's decision concerning the objectives of representation, including whether or not to accept an offer to settlement, and will endeavor to explain any matter to the extent reasonably necessary to permit the client to make informed decisions regarding representation. During the course of representation and afterwards, the counsel may not use or reveal a client's confidence or secrets, except as required or permitted by law.

(3)   **COMMUNICATION.** The counsel will keep the client reasonably informed about the status of representation and will promptly respond to reasonable requests for information, including any reasonable request for an estimate respecting future costs of the representation or an appropriate portion of it. The client shall be truthful in all discussions with the counsel and provide all information or documentation required to enable the counsel to provide competent representation. During

representation, the client is entitled to receive all pleadings and substantive documents prepared on behalf of the client and every document received from any other counsel of record. At the end of the representation and on written request from the client, the counsel will return to the client all original documents and exhibits. In the event that the counsel withdraws from representation, or is discharged by the client, the counsel will turn over to the substituting counsel (or, if no substitutions, to the client) all original documents and exhibits together with complete copies of all pleadings and discovery within thirty (30) days of the counsel's withdrawal or discharge.

(4)   **ETHICAL CONDUCT**. The counsel cannot be required to engage in conduct which is illegal, unethical, or fraudulent. In matters involving minor children, the counsel may refuse to engage in conduct which, in the counsel's professional judgment, would be contrary to the best interest of the client's minor child or children. A counsel who cannot ethically abide by his client's direction shall be allowed to withdraw from representation.

(5)   **FEES**. The counsel's fee for services may not be contingent upon the securing of a dissolution of marriage, upon obtaining custody, or be based upon the amount of maintenance, child support, or property settlement received, except as specifically permitted under Supreme Court rules. The counsel may not require a non-refundable retainer fee, but must remit back any overpayment at the end of the representation. The counsel may enter into consensual security arrangement with the client whereby assets of the client are pledged to secure payment or legal fees or costs, but only if the counsel first obtains approval of the Court. The counsel will prepare and provide the client with an itemized billing statement detailing hourly rates (and/or other criteria), time spent, tasks performed, and costs incurred on a regular basis, at least quarterly. The client should review each billing statement promptly and address any objection or error in a timely manner. The client will not be billed for time spent to explain or correct a billing statement. If an appropriately detailed written estimate is submitted to a client as to future costs for a counsel's representation or a portion of the contemplated services (i.e., relative to specific steps recommended by the counsel in the estimate)

and, without objection from the client, the counsel then performs the contemplated services, all such services are presumptively reasonable and necessary, as well as to be deemed pursuant to the client's direction. In an appropriate case, the client may pursue contribution to his fees and costs from the other party.

(6)   **DISPUTES.** The counsel-client relationship is regulated by the Illinois Rules of Professional Conduct (Article VIII of the Illinois Supreme Court Rules), and any dispute shall be reviewed under the terms of such Rules.

APPENDIX E

RETAINER AGREEMENT AND FEE CONTRACT

THIS AGREEMENT is made this _____ day of _____, _____, and between _____, hereinafter designated as the CLIENT, and MARK D. BRENT of the DRENDEL & JANSONS LAW GROUP, hereinafter designated as the ATTORNEY, as follows:

1.   The CLIENT has retained and does hereby retain and employ the ATTORNEY to act for and on behalf of the CLIENT in connection   with   the   following   legal   matter:

_____

_____

_____

2.   The ATTORNEY reserves the right to delegate work on this matter to appropriate support staff or attorneys with the firm of DRENDEL & JANSONS LAW GROUP. Although the lawyer with primary responsibility for this file will take responsibility for the majority of the work hereunder, in appropriate situations, other attorneys or staff may provide work under this contract.

3.   The CLIENT agrees to cooperate with the ATTORNEY by assisting in the investigation of this matter, providing all information known or available to the CLIENT, and by otherwise assisting the ATTORNEY with regard to this case.

4.   In consideration of the services rendered and to be rendered by the ATTORNEY, the CLIENT agrees to pay to the ATTORNEY a reasonable attorneys fee calculated as follows:

_____   a. A flat fee of $_____.

_____   b. A fee computed by multiplying the total number of hours devoted by the ATTORNEY or his delagees to the above described matter multiplied by an agreed hourly rate of $_____. Where appropriate, support staff time will be billed at the rate of $_____ per hour.

____   c. Other (Describe):
          Court and other costs are to be: _____

5.   (If applicable) the CLIENT agrees to pay a retainer in the amount of $_____ to apply to attorney's fees, costs and expenses in connection with the above matter. If funds remain following the ATTORNEY'S completion of representation, any unearned funds will be returned to the CLIENT.

6.   The CLIENT understands and agrees that for any fees calculated under the provision of paragraph 4b, the ATTORNEY will bill all telephone calls, letters and other services in connection with said item at a minimum rate of one-quarter hour each and that necessary travel time is billed at regular rates.

7.   In addition to the attorney's fees calculated in accordance with the foregoing, the CLIENT understands and agrees that the CLIENT is liable for all costs and expenses incurred by the ATTORNEY in connection with the handling of the above matter, regardless of the result.

8.   The parties agree that all attorney's fees, costs and expenses for which the CLIENT is liable by reason of the foregoing provision shall be billed to the CLIENT by the ATTORNEY as follows (check one):

____   a. at the conclusion of the matter for attorney's fees.

____   b. quarterly.

____   c. monthly.

____   d. bi-monthly.

_____ e. other (describe): All costs and expenses to be paid in advance.

9.   The CLIENT understands and agrees that any bill rendered to the CLIENT by the ATTORNEY pursuant to the provision of the foregoing paragraphs which remains unpaid, in whole or in part, for more than sixty (60) days after the date of such bill, shall bear interest on the unpaid balance at the rate of 1 1/2% per month until fully paid. Provided, however, that if said interest rate is determined to be in excess of the maximum interest rate permitted by law, then said rate of interest shall be reduced to the maximum rate of interest allowed by law and the CLIENT agrees to waive any claim for penalties which might otherwise be assessed by reason of the provision of any interest rate law, and the CLIENT further agrees to not accept the payment of any such penalties. It is agreed and understood by the parties hereto that fees which remain unpaid for sixty (60) days or more may, at the option of the ATTORNEY, result in the ATTORNEY seeking leave of Court to withdraw as counsel for the CLIENT. Should a dispute arise regarding the fee charged, the parties agree to refer said dispute to the Illinois State Bar Association's Voluntary Fee Arbitration committee for binding arbitration. The ATTORNEY reserves the right to file suit for amounts due, interest, court costs, and reasonable attorney's fees.

For cases filed or litigated in DuPage County, Illinois, the parties expressly waive the DuPage County Fee Arbitration system, in favor of the provisions of this contract. Neither party shall be bound by the terms of the DuPage County Fee Arbitration system, unless this provision is stricken and initialed; or, if the parties otherwise agree in writing to utilize the system.

10.   Pursuant to Law, this ATTORNEY has an attorney's lien on any claim arising out of this matter, and on any sums realized by the CLIENT by way of settlement or judgment.

11.   The ATTORNEY agrees to accept employment by the CLIENT in connection with the above matter on the basis above described and agrees to use his best efforts and perform all ethical

services and acts which, in the judgment of the ATTORNEY, are necessary and proper to enforce and protect the rights of the CLIENT in connection with the above matter. The ATTORNEY, however, cannot make and does not make any guarantee as to the result which will be obtained therein.

12.   This contract is to be interpreted under the laws of the State of Illinois. If any provision of this contract is declared invalid, the remaining provisions of the contract shall not be affected thereby.

13.   The CLIENT acknowledges receipt of a copy of the "Statement of Client's Rights and Responsibilities", pursuant to 750 ILCS 508(f).

14.   The CLIENT acknowledges and agrees that any retainer or other payment made to ATTORNEY by credit card will be subject to an additional $35 convenience and handling charge.

IN WITNESS WHEREOF the parties hereto have caused the above and foregoing Attorney's Fee Contract to be executed the day and year first above written.

CLIENT: ATTORNEY:

_____   By: _____
                                                 Mark D. Brent

APPENDIX F

LEGAL SERVICES AGREEMENT (LSA)

<Date>

<Client's name
and Address>

Re:

Dear <Client's name>:

Thank you for selecting Drendel & Jansons Law Group to represent you in your family law action. Illinois law contains procedures for us to formalize our relationship with you by a written engagement agreement. If you approve of this letter, it, combined with the Retainer Agreement, will constitute the engagement agreement between us. The letter explains our objectives and sets forth our fee arrangements in further detail. The statute provides that the written engagement agreement be entered into by you and our firm at the time you retain us, or reasonably soon thereafter.

Our work on your behalf can include: evaluation of the circumstances of your case, advice, discovery, investigation, analysis, research, negotiation, settlement, or, if necessary, litigation of your case to a final adjudication, which may also include appeals. All of these endeavors require careful prior preparation by us. Depending on the circumstances of your matter, the process to judgment may involve such issues as: children's custody, visitation, health, and education arrangements; distinguishing between marital and non-marital property; valuation, allocation, and assignment of property; dissipation of assets; determination of appropriate maintenance and children's support for you or for your spouse; and a decision of whether any of the attorneys' fees and costs that you have incurred can be shifted from you to your spouse, or vice versa. There may also be post-judgment matters. When elements of your case are outside of our expertise, it may be necessary to seek advice from an expert in the area of concern, for example, accounting matters, property valuation, or psychological evaluation.

Fees are based on the hourly charges described in the Retainer and Fee Agreement previously signed by you and on Exhibit "A" to this Agreement. You will be billed for all time spent in handling your case, including time spent waiting for a case to be called in court, travel time, and research. I will be primarily responsible for case. We use a "team" approach in our Firm, and other attorneys in our firm may handle matters related to your case as we consider best to provide prompt and efficient service to you.

Each attorney has a highly trained secretary or assistant available. You may leave messages with the secretary or assistant, and she may relay specific factual information such as court times, court room numbers, et cetera. The secretary or assistant cannot give legal advice. You are not billed for secretarial work, but you will be billed for paralegal services when performed by secretaries, assistants, or paralegals. We reserve the right to change any hourly rate on thirty (30) days written notice to you.

Some cases because of their unusual nature warrant a departure from hourly rate charges. Examples are cases involving novel issues, extraordinary time demands, the use of unique experience, unusual results, and the like. Any increase or decrease in our final fees above or below hourly rates will occur only in such circumstances, and then only with your specific agreement or by court order.

You will be billed for all time expended by each lawyer and paralegal who works on your case with time entries kept by the ¼ hours. Even a seemingly brief task like a letter or a phone call usually takes 15 minutes to complete as it is necessary for us to stop what we are doing, obtain the file or other documents from your file relating to the task, focus our attention on the facts and details of your matter, complete the particular tasks and keep notes on what has been done and what follow up is necessary. Your bills will include time expended for: consultations and meetings; telephone calls and written correspondence; research; analysis; preparation of pleadings, discovery requests, memoranda, briefs, agreements, judgments, and other court documents; discovery, including depositions, interrogatories, production and inspection of documents; negotiations; court appearances, including waiting time and travel; and lawyers' preparation. We reserve the right to bill a minimum amount for certain tasks based upon the value of the services provided to the client. For example, we may bill a minimum charge of one hour for drafting a pleading or attending a court appearance. You are responsible for all costs, which can include: filing fees, court reporter costs, copy fees, long distance telephone charges, travel costs, messenger fees, computerized research, facsimile transmissions, and the like. If it is necessary to employ outside experts, you will be responsible for their charges. Costs and expert fees and costs may be billed to you directly. You will receive monthly itemized billing statements from our office that set forth the time, charges, work performed, and costs incurred by us.

You <have paid our firm> <will pay our firm with the delivery of this letter> a retainer of $<amount>. The retainer will be placed in our trust account and will be credited against the legal fees incurred on your behalf. In the event it appears that there will be a contested trial, you may be required to pay an additional retainer, in an amount to be agreed upon, to cover the anticipated attorneys' fees and costs of the trial. Any unused portion of the retainer fee will be refunded to you at the conclusion of our representation of you. The Retainer Agreement that you received and signed, along with the Statement of Client's Rights and Responsibilities are hereby incorporated into and have become a part of this agreement.

Any balances reflected in a monthly statement will be charged to your retainer payment. If your retainer balance reaches $0 you will receive a letter requesting that you replenish your retainer and specifying an amount. If payment is not received by our office within fourteen (14) days and if other arrangements have not been agreed upon in writing between this firm and yourself, we reserve the following rights:

(a) to terminate our attorney/client relationship for non-payment of fees or costs; and/or

(b) to take whatever action necessary to collect monies owed us.

(c) In the event of termination of our employment as your attorneys, you shall be responsible for all of the firm's costs of collection, including all legal expenses and costs.

If in any month you do not receive a bill or have a question concerning your bill, please let us know immediately. One reason for billing on a monthly basis is to give you an opportunity to bring any problems relating to your bill to our immediate attention and to inform you as to the accruing charges. Review your bills carefully upon receipt. Any objection you may have with regard to your billing must be communicated in writing within a thirty (30) day period; otherwise, all objections to our charges will be deemed waived. Interest will be charged at nine percent (9%) for unpaid fees and costs if the retainer deposit has been exhausted, and after thirty (30) days from billing date. The interest will show on your statement.

You are responsible for your own attorneys' fees and costs. Depending on your financial circumstances, those of your spouse, and the outcome of the litigation, we may seek to obtain payment of all or part of your fees and costs by your spouse. Conversely, your spouse may attempt to obtain payment from you for fees and costs. Payment of the fees and costs of one spouse by the other may be sought from time to time during the progress of your case on an interim basis, and, finally, on a permanent basis. Payment of a portion of one party's fees and costs by the other party on a permanent basis is called "contribution" by the statute. Although you each have a right to seek interim fees and permanent contribution from the other, you should understand that you are responsible for fees and costs that you incur that are not paid by your spouse. You are responsible for all of the fees and costs incurred in your matter regardless of the outcome of your case.

For cases filed or litigated in DuPage County, Illinois, the parties expressly waive the DuPage County Fee Arbitration system, in favor of the provisions of this contract. Neither party shall be bound by the terms of the DuPage County Fee Arbitration system unless this provision is stricken and initialed; or, if the parties otherwise agree in writing to utilize the system. Should a dispute arise regarding the fee charged, the

Firm reserves the right to refer said dispute to the Illinois State Bar Association's Voluntary Fee Arbitration committee for binding arbitration. The attorney also reserves the right to file suit for amounts due, interest, court costs, and reasonable attorney's fees.

Following our representation of you, the documents that constitute your file will be retained and stored by our office for at least seven (7) years. Thereafter the file may be destroyed. Please advise us in writing if you would like your file to be returned to you after our representation of you has concluded.

If any questions whatsoever remain unanswered concerning this engagement letter, the Retainer Agreement or the attached "Statement of Client's Rights and Responsibilities," please contact me at your first convenience. After you have read and fully understood this letter, if you are satisfied with it, kindly sign the enclosed copy of the letter on the line indicated by your name, and return the copy to me. Retain the original copy in your files. The letter will then constitute the engagement agreement between us.

We look forward to representing you.

Sincerely yours,

DRENDEL & JANSONS LAW GROUP

XXX/xxx   <attorney>
Enclosures

I have read the foregoing engagement agreement; I understand it; I am satisfied with it; and I accept its terms.

Dated: _____   _____

APPENDIX G

STIPULATION FOR WAIVER

THE CIRCUIT COURT OF THE
SIXTEENTH JUDICIAL CIRCUIT
KANE COUNTY, ILLINOIS

IN RE THE MARRIAGE OF:)   **GEN. NO.**
)
_____,   )
)
      Petitioner,   )
)
   and   )
)
_____,   )
)
      Respondent.   )

STIPULATION FOR WAIVER

The Petitioner, _____, and the Respondent, _____, hereby stipulate as follows:

1.   That they are Husband and Wife having been married the ____ day of _____, _____.

2.   That they have lived separate and apart since _____, a continuous period not less than six (6) months.

3.   That there has been an irretrievable breakdown of their marriage and it is their desire to obtain a Judgment for Dissolution of Marriage without proof of fault, and they hereby waive and relinquish the two (2) year requirement of living separate and apart.

4.   That this waiver is being made knowingly and without coercion. That each has been given the opportunity to seek the advice of counsel and that each wishes to be bound by this waiver.

We hereunto set our hands this _____ day of _____, 2012.

_____   _____

Petitioner, _____   Respondent, _____

Prepared by:
Mark D. Brent

APPENDIX H

INTERROGATORIES

IN THE CIRCUIT COURT OF THE
SIXTEENTH JUDICIAL CIRCUIT
KANE COUNTY, ILLINOIS

IN RE THE MARRIAGE OF:	)	**GEN. NO.** _____
	)	
_____,	)	
Petitioner,	)	
	)	
and	)	
	)	
_____,	)	
Respondent.	)	

<u>INTERROGATORIES</u>

NOW COMES, _____, by his counsel, Mark D. Brent of the DRENDEL & JANSONS LAW GROUP, and requests that the following Interrogatories be answered by _____, Respondent, under oath, within twenty-eight (28) days from the date of service hereof in accordance with Illinois Supreme Court Rule 213 and the applicable provisions of the Illinois Civil Practice Act.

1.   State your name, address, date of birth, Social Security Number, and driver's license number.
ANSWER:

2.   List all employment held by you during the preceding five (5) years and with regard to each employment, state:
        a.   The name and address of each employer;
        b.   Your position, job title or description;
        c.   If you had an employment contract;

d.   The date on which you commenced your employment and, if applicable, the date and reason for the termination of your employment;

e.   Your current gross and net income per pay period;

f.   Your gross income as shown on the last W-2 tax and wage statement received by you, your social security wages as shown on the last W-2 tax and wage statement received by you, and the amounts of all deductions shown thereon; and

g.   All additional benefits or perquisites received from your employment stating the type and value thereof.

ANSWER:

3.   During the preceding five (5) years, have you had any source of income other than from your employment listed above? If so, with regard to each source of income, state the following:

a.   The source of income, including the type of income and name and address of the source;

b.   The frequency in which you receive income from the source;

c.   The amount of income received by you from the source during the immediately preceding five (5) years; and

d.   The amount of income received by you from the source for each month during the immediately preceding five (5) years;

ANSWER:

4.   Do you own any interest in real estate? If so, with regard to each such interest state the following:

a.   The size and description of the parcel of real estate, including improvements thereon;

b.   The name, address and interest of each person who has or claims to have an ownership;

c.   The date your interest in the parcel of real estate was acquired;

d.   The consideration you transferred or paid for your interest in the parcel of real estate;

e.   Your estimate of the current fair market value of the parcel of real estate and your interest therein; and

f.   The amount of any indebtedness owed on the parcel of real estate and to whom;

ANSWER:

5.   For the preceding five (5) years, list the names and addresses of all associations, partnerships, corporations, enterprises or entities in which you have an interest or claim any interest, the nature of your interest or claim of interest therein, the amount of percentage of your interest or claim of interest therein, and an estimate of the value of your interest therein.

ANSWER:

6.   During the preceding five (5) years, have you had any account or investment in any type of financial institution, individually or with another or in the name of another, including checking accounts, savings accounts, certificates of deposit and money market accounts? If so, with regard to each such account or investment, state the following:

a.   The type of account or investment;

b.   The name and address of the financial institution;

c.   The name and address of each person in whose name the account is held; and

d.   Both the high and the low balance of the account or investment, stating the date of the high balance and the date of the low balance.

ANSWER:

7.   During the preceding five (5) years, have you been the holder of or had access to any safety deposit boxes? If so, state the following:

      a.   The name of the bank or institution where such box is located;

      b.   The number of each box;

      c.   A description of the contents of each box during the immediately preceding five (5) years and as of the date of the answer; and

      d.   The name and address of any joint or co-owners of such safety deposit box or any trustees holding the box for your benefit.

ANSWER:

8.   During the immediately preceding five (5) years, has any person or entity held cash or property on your behalf? If so, state:

      a.   The name and address of the person or entity holding the cash or property; and

      b.   The type of cash or property held and the value thereof.

ANSWER:

9.   During the preceding five (5) years, have you owned any stocks, bonds, securities or other investments, including savings bonds? If so, which regard to each such stock, bond, security or investment state:

      a.   A description of the stock, bond, security or investment;

      b.   The name and address of the entity issuing the stock, bond, security or investment;

      c.   The present value of such stock, bond, security or investment;

      d.   The date of acquisition of the stock, bond, security or investment;

      e.   The cost of the stock, bond, security or investment;

    f.   The name and address of any other owner or owners in such stock, bond, security or investment; and

    g.   If applicable, the date sold and the amount realized therefrom.

ANSWER:

    5.   Do you own or have any incidents of ownership in any life, annuity or endowment insurance policies? If so, with regard to each such policy state:

    a.   The name of the company;

    b.   The number of the policy;

    c.   The face value of the policy;

    d.   The present value of the policy;

    e.   The amount of any loan or encumbrance on the policy;

    f.   The date of acquisition of the policy; and

    g.   With regard to each policy, the beneficiary or beneficiaries.

ANSWER:

    11.   Do you have any right, title, claim or interest in or to a pension plan, retirement plan or profit sharing plan, including, but not limited to, individual retirement accounts, 401(k) plans and deferred compensation plans? If so, with regard to each such plan state:

    a.   The name and address of the entity providing the plan;

    b.   The date of your initial participation in the plan; and

    c.   The amount of funds currently held on your behalf under the plan.

ANSWER:

12.   Do you have any outstanding indebtedness or financial obligations, including mortgages, promissory notes, or other oral or written contracts?   If so, with regard to each obligation state the following:

    a.   The name and address of the creditor;
    b.   The form of the obligation;
    c.   The date the obligation was initially incurred;
    d.   The amount of the original obligation;
    e.   The purpose or consideration for which the obligation was incurred;
    f.   A description of any security connected with the obligation;
    g.   The rate of interest on the obligation;
    h.   The present unpaid balance of the obligation;
    i.   The dates and amounts of installment payments; and
    j.   The date of maturity of the obligation.

ANSWER:

13.   Are you owed any money or property? If so, state:
    a.   The name and address of the debtor;
    b.   The form of the obligation;
    c.   The date the obligation was initially incurred;
    d.   The amount of the original obligation;
    f.   The description of any security connected with the obligation;
    g.   The rate of interest on the obligation;
    h.   The present unpaid balance of the obligation;
    i.   The dates and amounts of installment payments; and
    j.   The date of maturity of the obligation.

ANSWER:

14.   State the year, make and model of each motor or motorized vehicle, motor or mobile home and farm machinery or equipment in which

you have an ownership, estate, interest or claim of interest, whether individually or with another, and with regard to each item state:

- a.   The date the item was acquired;
- b.   The consideration paid for the item;
- c.   The name and address of each other person who has a right, title, claim or interest in or to the item;
- d.   The approximate fair market value of the item; and
- e.   The amount of any indebtedness on the item and the name and address of the creditor.

ANSWER:

15.   Have you purchased or contributed towards the payment for or provided other consideration or improvement with regard to any real estate, motorized vehicle, financial account or securities, or other property, real or personal, on behalf of another person or entity other than your spouse during the preceding five (5) years? If so, with regard to each such transaction state:

- a.   The name and address of the person or entity to whom you contributed;
- b.   The type of contribution made by you;
- c.   The type of property to which the contribution was made;
- d.   The location of the property to which the contribution was made;
- e.   Whether or not there is written evidence of the existence of a loan; and
- f.   A description of the written evidence.

ANSWER:

16. During the preceding five (5) years, have you made any gift of cash or property, real or personal, to any person or entity not your spouse? If so, with regard to each such transaction state:

- a.   A description of the gift;
- b.   The value of the gift;

    c.   The date of the gift;

    d.   The name and address of the person or entity receiving the gift;

    e.   Whether or not there is written evidence of the existence of a gift; and

    f.   A description of the written evidence.

ANSWER:

17.   During the preceding five (5) years, have you made any loans to any person or entity not your spouse and, if so, with regard to each such loan state:

    a.   A description of the loan;

    b.   The value of the loan;

    c.   The date of the loan;

    d.   The name and address of the person or entity receiving the loan;

    e.   Whether or not there is written evidence of the existence of a loan; and

    f.   A description of the written evidence.

ANSWER:

18.   During the preceding five (5) years, have you sold, transferred, conveyed, encumbered, concealed, damaged or otherwise disposed of any property owned by you and/or your spouse individually or collectively? If so, with regard to each item or property state:

    a.   A description of the property;

    b.   The current location of the property;

    c.   The purpose or reason for the action taken by you with regard to the property;

    d.   The approximate fair market value of the property;

    e.   Whether or not there is written evidence of any such transaction; and

    f.   A description of the written evidence.

ANSWER:

19.   During the preceding five (5) years, have any appraisals been made with regard to any of the property listed by you under your answers to these interrogatories? If so, state:

    a.   The name and address of the person conducting each such appraisal;

    b.   A description of the property appraised;

    c.   The date of the appraisal; and

    d.   The location of any copies of each such appraisal.

ANSWER:

20.   During the preceding five (5) years, have you prepared or has anyone prepared for you any financial statements, net worth statements or lists of assets and liabilities pertaining to your property or financial affairs? If so, with regard to each such document state:

    a.   The name and address of the person preparing each such document;

    b.   The type of document prepared;

    c.   The date the document was prepared; and

    d.   The location of all copies of each such document.

ANSWER:

21.   State the name and address of any accountant, tax preparer, bookkeeper and other person, firm or entity who has kept or prepared books, documents and records with regard to your income, property, business or financial affairs during the course of this marriage.
ANSWER:

22.   List all non-marital property claimed by you, identify each item of property as to the type of property, the date received, the basis on which you claim it is non-marital property, its location, and the present value of the property.
ANSWER:

23.   List all martial property of this marriage, identifying each item of property as to the type of property, the basis on which you claim it to be marital property, its location, and the present value of the property.
ANSWER:

24.   What contribution or dissipation has your spouse made to the marital estimate, including but not limited to each of the items or property identified in response to interrogatories No. 22 and No. 23 above, citing specifics, if any, for each item of property?
ANSWER:

25.   Pursuant to Illinois Supreme Court Rule 213(f), provide the name and address of each witness who will testify at trial and state the subject of each witness' testimony.
ANSWER:

26.   Pursuant to Illinois Supreme Court Rule 213(g), provide the name and address of each opinion witness who will offer any testimony, and state:

    a.   The subject matter on which the opinion witness is expected to testify;

    b.   The conclusions and/or opinions of the opinion witness and the basis therefor, including reports of the witness, if any;

    c.   The qualifications of each opinion witness, including a *curriculum vitae* and/or resume, if any; and

    d.   The identity of any written reports of the opinion witness regarding this occurrence.

ANSWER:

27.   Are you in any manner incapacitated or limited in your ability to earn income at the present time? If so, define and describe such incapacity or limitation, and state when such incapacity or limitation commenced and when it is expected to end.
ANSWER:

28.   Identify any statements, information and/or documents known to you and requested by any of the foregoing interrogatories which you claim to be work product or subject to any common law or statutory privilege, and with respect to each interrogatory, specify the legal basis for the claim as required by Illinois Supreme Court Rule 201(n).
ANSWER:

DRENDEL & JANSONS LAW GROUP

By: _____
        Mark D. Brent

ATTESTATION

STATE OF _____   )

) SS

COUNTY OF _____   )

_____, being first duly sworn on oath, deposes and states that he/she is the Petitioner/Respondent in the above-captioned matter, that he/she has read the foregoing document, and the answers made herein are true, correct and complete to the best of his/her knowledge and belief.

_____

<Opponent's typed name w/signature above>

Subscribed and Sworn to before me this
_____ day of _____, _____.

_____

Notary Public

APPENDIX I

REQUEST FOR PRODUCTION OF DOCUMENTS

IN THE CIRCUIT COURT OF THE
SIXTEENTH JUDICIAL CIRCUIT
KANE COUNTY, ILLINOIS

IN RE THE MARRIAGE OF:	) **GEN. NO.** _____
	)
_____,	)
Petitioner,	)
	)
and	)
	)
_____,	)
Respondent.	)

REQUEST FOR PRODUCTION OF DOCUMENTS

TO: _____

c/o Attorney _____

_____

_____

You are hereby notified that, pursuant to Supreme Court Rule 213, you are requested to produce on a date and at a time no later than twenty-eight (28) days from the date of the filing of this Notice, at the DRENDEL & JANSONS LAW GROUP, 111 Flinn Street, Batavia, Illinois, attorney for the Petitioner, for inspection and copying the following documents (as the term is defined in Illinois Supreme Court Rule 201) together with any transcripts, reports, memoranda or recordings purporting to reflect, but not to evaluate the same.

It is further requested that if any type of privilege is being asserted or if any records are being withheld for any reason, that the type of record withheld and the basis for the privilege be specifically stated in the response to this notice.

If you are not in possession of the items requested, you are directed to disclose any information that you have which is calculated to lead to the discovery of the whereabouts of any of these items, specifying the location where the item may be found, the name(s) of the person having possession, and the relationship between any party and the possessor of the item.

REQUEST FOR PRODUCTION OF DOCUMENTS

ASSETS

1.   All financial statements, loan applications, promissory notes, security agreements, and lines of credit filed, submitted, or drawn up in the last five (5) years for, or on the behalf of you, your business, or any business in which you are involved to any degree of ownership, management, or control. To the extent you are unable to produce a financial statement, set out where a copy of said statement can be obtained. This would include, but not be limited to, any financial statements prepared by financial planners, accountants, and so on.

2.   All documents that evidence any degree of ownership, actual or beneficial, in real estate, including, but not limited to, Warranty Deeds, Quit Claim Deeds, and Deeds of Trust, Mortgages, leases, and any transfer of any kind in any degree for the last five (5) years. Include also any document which may in any way have any bearing on the value thereof now or in the future.

3.   All documents that evidence ownership, control, or indebtedness such as stock certificates, partnership agreements, bonds, loans, or any other agreements that evidence any ownership or control or indebtedness that you have in or from any business interest, whether it be a corporation, partnership, sole proprietorship, or other. Include any such interest transferred in any way by you in the last five (5) years. This includes stock in companies in which you have essentially no control. Also include any documents that may be reasonably deemed to

have a bearing on the value now or in the future of the ownership, including, but not limited to, buy-sell agreements, corporate minutes, books, records, articles of incorporation, corporate charters, certificates of authority, valuations, stock subscription agreements, by-laws, and stock restrictions.

4.   All documents that reflect the income, expenses, assets, liabilities, or value for any corporation or business entity in which you have or have had any interest during the past five (5) years, including, but not limited to:

> income tax returns,
> balance sheets,
> profit and loss statements,
> general ledgers,
> payroll ledgers,
> depreciation schedules,
> corporate minutes,
> financial statements,
> income statements, and
> buy\sell agreements.

5.   All documents relating to any interests that you have or may have had for any time in the last five (5) years, in any:

> salary or non-salary pension plan,
> profit-sharing plan,
> IRA,
> deferred compensation,
> 401(K) plan,
> employee stock ownership plan,
> patent,
> copyright,
> invention,
> royalty,
> brokerage firm accounts,
> annuities,

stocks,
bonds,
mortgages, or
leases.

This would include, but is not limited to,

plan benefit summaries,
beneficiary designations,
benefit account,
insurance plans,
travel plans,
expense accounts,
discount plans, and
bonuses or stock options.

6. All documents that reflect the name, location, number, and contents and transactions from any accounts in a bank, savings and loan, brokerage house, or other institution in your name or in the names of others or to which you have or have had access during the past five (5) calendar years and statements from same for the last five (5) years. All canceled checks (front and back), check register, check stub, deposit slips, debit or credit memoranda, transaction advices, and bank statements for all bank accounts, liquid asset accounts, or other accounts that you have been authorized to write checks on or had any involvement with during the last five (5) years. All documents relating to the name, location, number, and content of any safety-deposit boxes rented by you or others to which you have or have had access to during the past five (5) calendar years.

7. All annuities and life insurance policies that are in effect upon your life or your spouse or have been for the last five (5) years. If the policies are group policies, produce documentation or booklets that describe said policies. Also provide information on any loans on said policies. This includes, but is not limited to, "face pages" or portions of the policy showing coverage, cash value, insured, and beneficiaries.

8.   All documents that show any right, interest, or prospect of pecuniary advantage or liability under any contract, agreement, or document now, in the future, or in the last five (5) years.

9.   All documents that reflect any lawsuit, deposition, claim, cause of action, or judgment in which you have been a party or in which you have participated in any degree for the last five (5) years.

10.   All documents evidencing any will, trust, annuity, estate, or other entity of which you are or have been in any degree a grantor, trustee, or beneficiary for the last five (5) years. This would include, but not be limited to, wills with all codicils, trust documents, tax returns, bank statements, checks, and court filings.

11.   All documents including, but not limited to, financial statements, appraisals, insurance policies, coverage schedules, titles and contracts for loans that reflect any item or collection of property over $500.00 in value owned by you not heretofore requested including, but not limited to:

> real estate,
> stocks,
> bonds,
> businesses,
> bank accounts,
> retirement plans,
> pensions,
> insurance,
> collections,
> jewelry,
> furs,
> cars,
> guns,
> art,
> books,
> furniture,
> automobiles,

contracts,
leases,
royalties,
copyrights,
patents,
debts owing you,
promissory notes,
mortgages,
certificates of deposits,
boats,
airplanes,
patents,
copyrights,
inventions, or
other collections

12.   All documents that reflect any money or property (over $500 in value) you brought into the marriage or that was given by you or received by you as a gift or inheritance before or during the marriage. This includes, but is not limited to, any property that you claim as your separate property and the value of said property. This includes, but is not limited to, inheritance, tax returns, gift tax returns, probate accountings, and specifically includes any property you claim as your separate property.

13.   All documents reflecting any:

offers,
inquiries,
discussions,
proposals, or
agreements

regarding any significant creation, sale, purchase, or any change in value, ownership, or status of any assets, liabilities, employment, source of income, or source of expense.

DEBTS

14.   All documents that reflect any debts that you owe or have owed for the last five (5) years. All charge accounts, debit or credit card charge slips, charge sheets, and statements that you have had during the past five (5) years.

INCOME

15.   All documents showing your gross income and other earnings for the current year and past five (5) years, including, but not limited to,

> contracts for employment,
> deferred compensation agreements,
> financial statements,
> income tax returns and all schedules,
> W-2 forms,
> other federal income reporting documents,
> leases,
> dividend statements,
> mortgages,
> checks or check stubs from any employer that reflect your gross income, deductions,
> bonuses,
> automobile allowances,
> commissions,
> trusts, and
> other earnings including trades for the current year and past five (5) years.

If any tax return has not been filed in the last five (5) years, please produce in its place your Request for Extension of Time to File and all documents filed with said request.

16.   Any and all documents reflecting your travel, food, lodging, entertainment, cleaning, and automobile or other expenses that

you received reimbursement for during the last twelve (12) months; also produce vouchers or other documentation relative to reimbursement for such expenses.

EXPENSES

17.   All documents showing your expenses for the past twelve (12) months, including, but not limited to, the lease at your place of residence, bills, statements, or other documentation showing cost of utilities, telephone, household furnishings, groceries, clothing, cleaning, car note, car license, inspection and city sticker, gasoline cost, car repair, tires, car insurance and other insurance costs, school tuition and registration fees, school supplies and books, gifts, recreation, doctor bills, dental bills, bill or statements of attorney's fees, retirement, lunch costs, and veterinarian bills.

18.   All health, accident, disability, and hospitalization policies that are in effect and cover you or any member of your family.

19.   All telephone bills for any phone you used or paid for the last five (5) years, including, but not limited to, all service charge orders.

20.   Any document that describes the terms upon which you are compensating your attorney. That includes, but is not limited to, the contract for representation and all bills on statements you have received from your attorney and any document that would show the source of those funds.

OTHER

21.   All photographs, letters, statements, recordings, videotapes, audiotapes, documents, and tangible things that would support you or your spouse's position on the issues of this case including, but not limited to, grounds or economic issues to which your spouse was a party or participant. This specifically includes any item you will attempt to introduce at trial or in depositions.

22.   All documents including, but not limited to, calendars, diaries, logs, journals, resumes, letters, and memorandums you have kept or used for the past five (5) that show your activities of a personal or business nature or could be used as a recording of past recollection or for the purpose of refreshing the recollection of any potential witness in this case.

23.   All documents or things given to, consulted or used by, any person who has investigated or has knowledge of any matter relating to the case including, but not limited to, any expert witness and any detective or investigator and copies of any reports, photographs, recordings, or documents generated or consulted by said person including, but not limited to, all reports, drafts, notes, and computations. This includes, but is not limited to, reports by physicians, psychiatrists, and psychologists on the physical, mental, or emotional condition of the parties and their children.

24.   All documents referred to in, relied on or upon, or which prove or support your answers to Interrogatories.

Please remember that this request is continuing in nature and that you are required to supplement it and all the above requests with such additional documents that you have access to in the future.

_____

Mark D. Brent, Attorney for _____

IRMO _____
CASE NO.
            _____ **COUNTY, IL**

STATE OF ILLINOIS) ss.
COUNTY OF KANE)

PROOF OF SERVICE

The undersigned, being duly sworn, says that on _____, a copy of the Request for Production of Documents was served on the following:

       Mr. or Ms. _____
       c/o Attorney _____
       _____
       _____
       _____

_____ By personally delivering a copy thereof to each party or person, addressed as above.

__X__ By depositing a copy thereof, enclosed in an envelope, in the United States Mail at Geneva or Batavia, Illinois, by First Class Mail, with proper postage prepaid, before the hour of 6:00 p.m., addressed as above.

_____ By faxing a copy to the above-named party at _____.

          _____

Subscribed and sworn to before me this
_____ day of _____, 2012.

_____
    NOTARY PUBLIC

APPENDIX J

INVOICE/STATEMENT

DRENDEL & JANSONS LAW GROUP
111 FLINN STREET
Batavia, IL 60510
Phone No. (630) 406-5440
Fax No. (630) 406-6179
E-mail
Tax Id No.
PLEASE SEND ALL PAYMENTS TO THE BATAVIA ADDRESS

Page: 1

ACCOUNT NO:
STATEMENT NO:

Fees Through

		HOURS	
09/28/2011			
MDB	Prepare correspondence to client re: engagement; prepare correspondence to client re: KIDS class.	0.50	150.00
MDB	Prepare Petition for Dissolution of Marriage; Summons; and New Case Information Sheet.	1.00	300.00
MDB	Prepare Petition for Interim Custody and Petition for Interim Relief.	1.50	450.00
MDB	Prepare Request for Comprehensive Financial Statement.	0.25	75.00
MDB	Office conference with client re: pleadings.	0.25	75.00
	FOR CURRENT SERVICES RENDERED	3.50	1,050.00

RECAPITULATION

Timekeeper	Title	Hours	Hourly Rate	TOTAL
Mark D. Brent		3.50	$300.00	$1,050.00

09/29/2011	Clerk of the Circuit Court filing fee.		236.00
	TOTAL EXPENSES		236.00
	TOTAL CURRENT WORK		1,286.00
09/30/2011	TRANSFERRED FROM TRUST		-500.00
	BALANCE DUE		$786.00

Client Funds

09/27/2011	PAYMENT RECEIVED. THANK YOU.	500.00
09/30/2011	PAYMENT TRANSFERRED FROM TRUST. THANK YOU.	-500.00

Ending Client Funds Balance $0.00

ABOUT THE AUTHOR

Attorney Mark Brent is a proud native of Aurora, Illinois, where he currently resides with his sons. Mark is a 1988 graduate of the University of Illinois (Bachelor of Arts/Rhetoric), and a 1991 graduate of the University of Illinois College of Law. Mark's scholastic honors include nomination to the Phi Beta Kappa Honor Society in college, scoring in the top 1 percent in the Law School Admissions Test (LSAT), and participating for two years on the University of Illinois' Moot Court Team in the field of product liability.

Mark began his legal career at the law firm of Williams Montgomery & John, in Chicago, Illinois, where he received extensive training and trial experience in many forms of litigation, including catastrophic death and injury cases, attorney and other professional malpractice cases, and insurance coverage/toxic tort litigation. Mark spent a decade as a solo practitioner, focusing his practice in family law over a five-county area in Chicagoland. He is now a member of the Drendel & Jansons Law Group, with offices in Batavia and Aurora, Illinois. Although a litigator throughout his entire twenty-plus year career, Mark's practice now focuses solely in the area of family law, with a heavy concentration in the areas of contested divorce and custody cases.

Outside the office, Mark's interests include Scouting, coaching football, travel, and the outdoors. In addition to this book, Mark has been a contributing author to our "Inside the Minds" series, writing on evolving custody trends in Illinois.

ASPATORE